Milady's Standard:
Nail Technology Workbook

Fourth Edition

STUDENT'S EDITION

Milady's Standard: Nail Technology Workbook

Fourth Edition

STUDENT'S EDITION

To be used with
MILADY'S STANDARD: NAIL TECHNOLOGY, FOURTH EDITION

Compiled by Linnea Lindquist
Revised by Sue Ellen Schultes

CENGAGE
Learning™

Austrailia   Canada   Mexico   Singapore   Spain   United Kingdom   United States

**Milady's Standard:
Nail Technology Workbook**

**Compiled by Linnea Lindquist
Revised by Sue Ellen Schultes**

For product information and technology assistance, contact us at
Cengage Learning Customer & Sales Support, 1-800-354-9706

For permission to use material from this text or product,
submit all requests online at **cengage.com/permissions**
Further permissions questions can be emailed to
permissionrequest@cengage.com

Library of Congress Control Number: 2002075308

ISBN-13: 978-1-56253-907-8

ISBN-10: 1-56253-907-8

Milady
5 Maxwell Drive
Clifton Park, NY 12065-2919
USA

Milady products are represented in Canada by Nelson Education, Ltd.

For your lifelong learning solutions, visit **milady.cengage.com**

Visit our corporate website at **cengage.com**

Notice to the Reader
Publisher does not warrant or guarantee any of the products described herein or perform any independent analysis in connection with any of the product information contained herein. Publisher does not assume, and expressly disclaims, any obligation to obtain and include information other than that provided to it by the manufacturer. The reader is expressly warned to consider and adopt all safety precautions that might be indicated by the activities described herein and to avoid all potential hazards. By following the instructions contained herein, the reader willingly assumes all risks in connection with such instructions. The publisher makes no representations or warranties of any kind, including but not limited to, the warranties of fitness for particular purpose or merchantability, nor are any such representations implied with respect to the material set forth herein, and the publisher takes no responsibility with respect to such material. The publisher shall not be liable for any special, consequential, or exemplary damages resulting, in whole or part, from the readers' use of, or reliance upon, this material.

Printed in the United States of America
9 10 11 12 13 12 11 10 09 08

Contents

How to Use This Workbook

Milady's Standard: Nail Technology Workbook has been written to meet the needs, interests, and abilities of students receiving training in nail technology.

This workbook should be used together with *Milady's Standard: Nail Technology.* This book follows the information found in the student textbook.

Students are to answer each item in this workbook with a pencil after consulting their textbook for correct information. Items can be corrected and/or rated during class or individual discussions, or on an independent study basis.

Various tests are included to emphasize essential facts found in the textbook and to measure the student's progress. Word Reviews are listed for each chapter. They are to be used as study guides, for class discussions, or for the teacher to assign groups of words to be used by the student in creative essays.

Introduction

1. List four advantages of becoming a nail technician in today's cosmetology profession.

   a. _____

   b. _____

   c. _____

   d. _____

2. This booming industry includes manicuring, _____, and _____.

3. The nail industry had a combined sales of more than _____ per year, which is an increase of more than _____ over previous years.

4. _____ is the key to excelling in the nail industry.

5. Besides becoming a nail technician, list five other career opportunities available to you.

   a. _____

   b. _____

   c. _____

   d. _____

   e. _____

6. The first manicure was recorded _____ years ago.

7. Discuss items nail technicians learn while in training for licensure.

   a. _____

   b. _____

   c. _____

   d. _____

   e. _____

   f. _____

8. a. What does the Latin word *manus* mean?

   _____

   b. What does the Latin word *cura* mean?

   _____

Part 1

GETTING STARTED

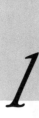

Your Professional Image

INTRODUCTION

1. The three groups of people that will be affected by rules for professional behavior are:

   a. _____.

   b. _____.

   c. _____.

2. List three elements that are included in the rules of professionalism.

   a. _____

   b. _____

   c. _____

PROFESSIONAL SALON CONDUCT

3. Define salon conduct.

   _____

   _____

4. Unprofessional behavior could affect your _____ , _____ and _____.

5. List thirteen items concerning salon conduct toward clients.

   a. _____

   b. _____

   c. _____

   d. _____

   e. _____

   f. _____

   g. _____

   h. _____

   i. _____

   j. _____

   k. _____

   l. _____

   m. _____

6. Being late is discourteous and can annoy and _____ your clients.

7. What four items should be included on an appointment schedule?

    a. _____

    b. _____

    c. _____

    d. _____

8. Schedule your appointments so that each client has enough _____.

9. a. List two situations when you should contact your clients about schedule changes.

    1. _____

    2. _____

    b. By contacting clients for the above two situations, your clients will:

    1. _____.

    2. _____.

10. List three aspects of a courteous attitude.

    a. _____

    b. _____

    c. _____

11. What six actions should be performed for a new client?

    a. _____

    b. _____

    c. _____

    d. _____

    e. _____

    f. _____

12. Explain why a nail technician should not chew gum, eat, or take personal phone calls where they can be seen by a client.

    _____

13. List thirteen items concerning salon conduct toward employers and coworkers.

    a. _____

    b. _____

    c. _____

    d. _____

    e. _____

    f. _____

    g. _____

    h. _____

    i. _____

    j. _____

    k. _____

l. _____

m._____

14. a. Problems or questions about your job should be discussed with your _____ .

    b. These problems or questions should not be discussed with your:

      1. _____ .

      2. _____ .

PROFESSIONAL ETHICS

15. Define professional ethics.

    _____

    _____

16. List four essential values when considering the feelings and rights of others.

    a. _____

    b. _____

    c. _____

    d. _____

17. Write down seven professional ethical behaviors toward clients.

    a. _____

    b. _____

    c. _____

    d. _____

    e. _____

    f. _____

    g. _____

18. Explain why a nail technician should not gossip about others to clients.

    _____

    _____

19. List five professional ethical behaviors with employers and coworkers.

    a. _____

    b. _____

    c. _____

    d. _____

    e. _____

YOUR PROFESSIONAL APPEARANCE

20. Give three reasons why you should be a model of good grooming.

    a. _____

    b. _____

    c. _____

21. List four actions of good grooming.

    a. _____

    b. _____

    c. _____

    d. _____

COMPLETION REVIEW

Insert the correct word listed in the sentences below.

appearance	coworkers	professional ethics
appointment schedule	employers	salon conduct
calendar	helpful	time
clients	inconvenience	

22. Being late is discourteous, and can annoy and _____ your clients.

23. The aspects of a courteous attitude include being cheerful, friendly, and _____.

24. The way you act when you are working with clients, your employer, and coworkers in a salon is called _____.

25. Schedule your appointments so that each client has enough _____.

26. Problems or questions about your job should be discussed with your _____.

27. Clients expecting you to look your best refers to your professional _____.

28. The client's name and phone number, service, and time should be included on a/an _____.

29. Your sense of right or wrong when you interact with your clients, employers, and coworkers is known as _____ .

WORD REVIEW

If you do not know the meanings of the words listed below, look them up in the text.

appearance	efficient	prepare
appointment schedule	employer	professional
argue	ethical standards	promote
communication	ethics	punctual
complain	fairness	respect
courteous	good grooming	rumors
courtesy	gossip	salon conduct
coworkers	honesty	
criticize	initiative	

Bacteria and Other Infectious Agents

INTRODUCTION

1. List four sources of infection.

   a. _____

   b. _____

   c. _____

   d. _____

2. List three agencies that can be accessed for help in discovering the possible problems of infectious agents pose.

   a. _____

   b. _____

   c. _____

BACTERIA

3. Define bacteria.

   _____

4. List some places where bacteria are found.

   a. _____

   b. _____

   c. _____

   d. _____

   e. _____

   f. _____

   g. _____

   h. _____

   i. _____

   j. _____

   k. _____

5. **Identification.** Using the letters **P** and **NP** (defined below), match the characteristics below with one type of bacteria.
   Key:
   P = pathogenic bacteria
   NP = nonpathogenic bacteria
   Characteristics:

   _____ a. less than 30% of all bacteria

   _____ b. are often beneficial

   _____ c. spread disease by producing toxins/poisons

   _____ d. help produce food and oxygen

   _____ e. in the mouth and intestines, they help the digestive process

   _____ f. nondisease-causing

   _____ g. 70% of all bacteria

   _____ h. harmful bacteria

   _____ i. cocci, bacilli, spirilla

   _____ j. most common cause of infection and disease

6. List four conditions in which bacteria live, grow, and multiply.

   a. _____

   b. _____

   c. _____

   d. _____

7. a. Define and explain mitosis.

   _____

   _____

   _____

   b. How many bacteria cells can be reproduced in 12 hours?

   _____

8. a. Define spore.

   _____

   _____

   b. When does this spore form?

   _____

   _____

   c. When will the bacteria grow and reproduce again?

   _____

   _____

9. **Identification.** Using the letters **C**, **B**, and **S** (defined below), match the characteristics below with one type of pathogenic bacteria.
   Key:
   C = cocci bacteria
   B = bacilli bacteria
   S = spirilla bacteria
   Characteristics:

   _____ a. the most common bacteria

   _____ b. causes influenza and typhoid

   _____ c. causes strep throat and blood poisoning

   _____ d. spiral-shaped

   _____ e. causes local infections such as boils

   _____ f. includes treponema pallida

   _____ g. rod-shaped

   _____ h. diplococci causes pneumonia

   _____ i. causes syphilis

   _____ j. corkscrew-shaped

   _____ k. round, pus-producing bacteria

   _____ l. causes tuberculosis and diphtheria

10. a. Which two types of bacteria can propel themselves?

    1. _____

    2. _____

    b. The hairlike projections by which they move are called _____ or _____ .

VIRUSES

11. Define viruses.

    _____

    _____

12. List in order the actions of viruses.

    a. _____

    b. _____

    c. _____

13. Viruses can be transformed through casual contact and spread when a person sneezes or

    _____ .

14. **Identification.** Using the letters **B** and **V** (defined below), match the diseases below with their cause.
    Key:
    B = bacteria-caused disease
    V = virus-caused disease
    Diseases:

    _____ a. pustules   _____ c. measles

    _____ b. common cold   _____ d. tetanus

_____ e. mumps   _____ h. chickenpox

_____ f. syphilis   _____ i. AIDS

_____ g. rheumatic fever   _____ j. strep throat

15. a. What do the letters AIDS stand for?

   _____

   b. What does the AIDS virus attack and eventually destroy?

   _____

   c. What are two common methods of transferring AIDS?

   1. _____

   2. _____

   d. What should you tell a client who is concerned about the spread of AIDS in the salon?

   _____

   _____

FUNGUS AND MOLD, PARASITES, AND RICKETTSIA

16. **Matching.** Match the terms on the left with their correct descriptions on the right.

   _____ 1. fungi

   _____ 2. mold

   _____ 3. rickettsia

   _____ 4. nail fungus

   _____ 5. parasites

   A. rarely, if ever, appears on fingernails; commonly confused with greenish bacterial infection

   B. causes AIDS and blood poisoning

   C. multicelled animal or plant organisms

   D. appears as a discoloration under the nail plate that spreads toward the cuticle

   E. one-celled plant microorganisms

   F. caused when the natural nail and products put on it are sanitized

   G. the general term for plant-like parasites

   H. causes typhus and Rocky Mountain spotted fever

17. a. Should a nail technician perform services on a client who has nail fungus?

   _____

   b. What should a nail technician do?

   _____

18. a. Explain what parasites live off.

   _____

   b. An example of a plant parasite is _____ .

   c. Animal parasites are responsible for contagious diseases. Three examples are:

   1. _____ .

   2. _____ .

   3. _____ .

19. Explain safety precautions that should be used when removing an artificial nail covering from a person who has a nail fungus or other infection.

    a. _____

    b. _____

    c. _____

    _____

    d. _____

    _____

    e. _____

UNDERSTANDING INFECTION

20. a. Explain when an infection occurs.

    _____

    _____

    b. At first, the infection is _____.

    c. If the infection spreads to the bloodstream, it is called a _____ infection.

21. **Matching.** Match the terms on the left with their correct descriptions on the right.

    _____ 1. immunity

    _____ 2. artificially acquired immunity

    _____ 3. general infection

    _____ 4. naturally acquired immunity

    _____ 5. localized infection

    _____ 6. natural immunity

    A. broken skin and lack of perspiration/bodily secretions

    B. ability of the body to resist disease and destroy microorganisms when they have entered the body

    C. often the first stage of an infection

    D. injection of serum or vaccine that introduces a small dose of disease-causing microorganisms into the body

    E. attacks and eventually destroys the body's immune system

    F. unbroken skin, natural secretions, and the blood's white blood cells

    G. after fighting off a disease, antibodies remain in the bloodstream

    H. the body's inability to resist disease-causing microorganisms

    I. example is blood poisoning

22. List five ways in which bacteria, viruses, and fungi enter the body.

    a. _____

    b. _____

    c. _____

    d. _____

    e. _____

23. List five common sources of becoming infected for a nail technician in the salon.

a. _____

b. _____

c. _____

d. _____

e. _____

24. Explain four ways nail technicians can fight infections.

a. _____

b. _____

c. _____

d. _____

25. List eight factors that contribute to the susceptibility of any individual in the contracting or spreading of infectious diseases.

a. _____

b. _____

c. _____

d. _____

e. _____

f. _____

g. _____

h. _____

MATCHING REVIEW

Insert the correct word listed in front of each definition below.

acquired immunity	immunity	pediculosis
AIDS	mitosis	ringworm
bacilli	natural immunity	scabies
bacteria	nonpathogenic	spirilla
cocci	parasites	spore
flagella	pathogenic	virus

26. _____ cell division

27. _____ common name for Acquired Immune Deficiency Syndrome

28. _____ type of bacteria that causes strep throat and blood poisoning

29. _____ multicelled animal or plant organisms

30. _____ one-celled microorganisms so small they can only be seen through a microscope

31. _____ bacteria move by these hair-like projections

32. _____ disease-causing agents that are many times smaller than bacteria

33. _____ a plant parasite that is contagious

34. _____ harmful bacteria including cocci, spirilla, and bacilli

35. _____ ability of the body to resist disease and destroy microorganisms when they have entered the body

36. _____ a tough outer covering on some bacteria

37. _____ spiral-shaped bacteria that causes syphilis

38. _____ nondisease causing, may be beneficial

39. _____ includes unbroken skin, natural secretions, and the blood's white blood cells

40. _____ rod-shaped bacteria

41. _____ another name for lice

WORD REVIEW

If you do not know the meanings of the words listed below, look them up in the text.

abscesses
Acquired Immune Deficiency
   Syndrome (AIDS)
artificially acquired immunity
animal organisms
asepsis
bacilli
bacteria
blood poisoning
boils
chickenpox
cilia
cocci
common cold
corkscrew
diplococci
diphtheria
disease-causing
dormant
flagella
fungi
fungus
general infection
germs
hepatitis

HIV virus
hypodermic needle
immune system
immunity
infection
influenza
itch-mite
lice
local infection
measles
microbes
microorganisms
mitosis
mold
mumps
nail fungus
natural immunity
naturally acquired immunity
nonpathogenic
parasites
pathogenic
pediculosis
plant organisms
plant parasite
pneumonia

poisons
pustules
rheumatic fever
rickettsia
ringworm
Rocky Mountain spotted fever
scabies
secretions
sepsis
spiral
spirilla
spore
staphylococci
strep throat
streptococci
syphilis
tetanus
toxins
treponema pallida
tuberculosis
typhoid
typhus
vaccine
virus

3

Sanitation and Disinfection

INTRODUCTION

1. Explain why states have strict rules for sanitation and disinfection procedures.

   _____

   _____

2. a. Define sterilize.

   _____

   b. Define sanitize.

   _____

   c. Define disinfection

   _____

   d. Of sterilize, sanitize, and disinfection which ones are possible in a salon?

   _____

DISINFECTION

3. Disinfection is the second level of _____ .

4. Disinfectants control microorganisms on _____ surfaces, but are not safe for use on

   _____

5. What items are listed on a Material Safety Data Sheet?

   a. _____

   b. _____

   c. _____

   d. _____

6. List three contaminants that a high-quality disinfectant must destroy.

   a. _____

   b. _____

   c. _____

7. List the five factors that contribute to the extent by which bacteria are killed.

   a. _____

   b. _____

   c. _____

d. _____

e. _____

8. U. V. sanitizers are useful _____ containers but the type sold to salons will not _____ salon implements.

9. Bead "sterilizers" do not _____ implements and are a _____ .

10. Formalin contains large amounts of formaldehyde. List five areas of the body it can irritate.

    a. _____

    b. _____

    c. _____

    d. _____

    e. _____

11. To clean up visible blood spills, many state cosmetology boards recommend

    _____

12. OSHA had adopted the standard of mandatory reporting of blood exposure incidents by the _____ to the _____ .

13. **Matching.** Match the terms on the left with their correct descriptions on the right.

    _____ 1. disinfection container   A.   is extremely flammable and evaporates quickly

    _____ 2. quats   B.   best for use when it appears cloudy

    _____ 3. phenolics   C.   the most cost effective of professional disinfectants

    _____ 4. alcohol   D.   best for disinfecting orangewood sticks

    _____ 5. bleach   E.   can discolor some materials and has almost no cleaning power

                                           F.   a glass, metal, or plastic container used to disinfect implements

                                           G.   has a high alkaline pH level

14. Why should a nail technician have at least two complete sets of implements?

    _____

15. a. Wash and rinse implements, then immerse them in hospital-level disinfectant for

    _____

    b. You and your client should use a _____ on your hands.

PRE-SERVICE SANITATION PROCEDURE

16. A manicuring table should be wiped with a/an _____ solution.

17. How often should the towel that is wrapped on a manicuring cushion be changed?

    _____

18. List four manicuring items that are to be discarded after use on one client.

    a. _____

    b. _____

c. _____

d. _____

19. What does it mean if the solution in your disinfection container is cloudy?

_____

DISINFECTION SAFETY

20. Name two protective items that should be worn when mixing or using disinfectants.

a. _____

b. _____

21. List five safety factors in working with disinfectants.

a. _____

b. _____

c. _____

d. _____

e. _____

22. List four important factors of Universal Sanitation.

a. _____

b. _____

c. _____

d. _____

MATCHING REVIEW

Insert the correct word listed in front of each definition below.

alcohol and bleach	formalin	sanitize
antiseptic	moist heat	sanitizers
disinfectant	phenolic	sterilize
disinfection container	quats	ultraviolet ray

23. _____ the most expensive common salon disinfectant

24. _____ useful for storing disinfected implements

25. _____ to destroy all living organisms on an object or surface

26. _____ contains a strong allergic sensitizer

27. _____ to reduce the number of pathogens on a surface

28. _____ cannot be diluted below 70% and remain effective

29. _____ holds a disinfectant solution so items can be submerged

30. _____ a substance that destroys pathogens on implements

31. _____ the common name for quaternary ammonium compounds

32. _____ reduce the number of pathogens in a cut

WORD REVIEW

If you do not know the meanings of the words listed below, look them up in the text.

alcohol

alkaline

allergic sensitizer

antibacterial

antiseptic

asthma

bactericide

bleach

bronchitis

contaminant

corrosion

decontamination

disinfectant

disinfection container

EPA

FDA

formaldehyde

formalin

fungicide

hepatitis B

hospital-level disinfectant

immersed

inhalation

Material Safety Data Sheet

pH

phenolics

quaternary ammonium
    compound

quats

residue

safety glasses

sanitize

sterilize

tongs

tuberculocidal disinfectant

ultraviolet ray sanitizer

Universal Sanitation

viricide

Safety in the Salon

INTRODUCTION

1. No products you use as a nail technician _____ harm your health, but all of them _____ .

COMMON CHEMICALS USED BY NAIL TECHNICIANS

2. List six chemical products commonly found on manicuring tables for technicians who perform advanced nail services.

   a. _____

   b. _____

   c. _____

   d. _____

   e. _____

   f. _____

3. Exposure to these chemicals won't harm you, but a danger you need to avoid is

   _____ .

4. List eleven early warning signs of overexposure to nail chemicals.

   a. _____

   b. _____

   c. _____

   d. _____

   e. _____

   f. _____

   g. _____

   h. _____

   i. _____

   j. _____

   k. _____

LEARN ABOUT THE CHEMICALS IN YOUR PRODUCTS

5. Whose responsibility is it to learn about the chemicals in products and how to handle them safely?

   _____

6. a. What do the letters MSDS stand for?

   _____

   b. To whom are product manufacturers required to make this sheet available?

   _____

   c. Where should they be kept?

   _____

7. List the fourteen items required on a MSDS.

   a. _____

   b. _____

   c. _____

   d. _____

   e. _____

   f. _____

   g. _____

   h. _____

   i. _____

   j. _____

   k. _____

   l. _____

   m. _____

   n. _____

8. List three ways products can enter your body.

   a. _____

   b. _____

   c. _____

9. The invisible sphere about the size of a beach ball that sits directly in front of your mouth is called your _____ .

10. List four easy and inexpensive ways to eliminate vapors from the salon.

    a. _____

    b. _____

    c. _____

    d. _____

11. The best form of salon vapor and dust control is _____ .

12. To protect your lungs, always wear a _____ when filing or drilling.

HOW TO PROTECT YOURSELF AND YOUR CLIENTS

13. **Figures.** Identify the safety precautions shown in the following figures.

a. _____

_____

b. _____

_____

c. _____

_____

d. _____

_____

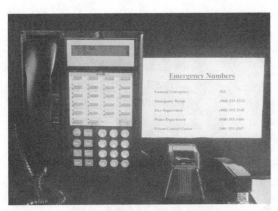

e. _____

_____

14. Explain why you should not store your lunch in the same refrigerator where chemical products are stored.

_____

15. If you forget to wash your hands before eating, you will probably end up _____ the
_____ on your hands.

16. Explain the effect of excessive heat on chemical products.

_____

17. a. How often should a nail technician's trash be emptied?

_____

b. Where should this trash be placed?

_____

18. What happens to each of the following if you forget to replace its cap?

a. nail polish _____

b. solvents _____

c. glue _____

CUMULATIVE TRAUMA DISORDERS

19. The most common cumulative trauma disorder is _____.

20. Seven symptoms of CTDs are:

a. _____

b. _____

c. _____

d. _____

e. _____

f. _____

g. _____

21. If you experience symptoms of CTD, _____ and _____
_____.

MATCHING REVIEW

Insert the correct word listed in front of each definition below.

absorption	glue	overexposure
beauty distributor	local exhaust	solvent
breathing zone	metal container with lid	ventilation
cumulative trauma disorder	MSDS	
flammable	nail polish	

22. _____ the invisible sphere about the size of a beach ball directly in front of your mouth

23. _____ where you can get MSDS

24. _____ the best form of salon dust and vapor control

25. _____ trash should be placed into this often

26. _____ uncapped, it evaporates

27. _____ Material Safety Data Sheet

28. _____ a system that removes vapors from the salon building

29. _____ early warning signs include watery eyes, light-headedness, and runny nose

30. _____ also known as repetitive motion disorder

31. _____ if left uncapped, it hardens

WORD REVIEW

If you do not know the meanings of the words listed below, look them up in the text.

absorb
acrylic liquid
acrylic powder
adhesive dryer
breathing zone
cancer
carcinogen
carpal tunnel syndrome
chemical hazards
contaminated
corrosive
cumulative trauma disorder
  (CTD)
dispose
dust mask
emergency
emergency numbers

expel
exposure
flammable
first aid
gel nail supplies
glue
harmful
hazards
HEPA
ibuprofen
ingestion
inhalation
insomnia
label
local exhaust
manufacturers

Material Safety Data Sheets
  (MSDS)
nail polish
overexposure
phenolic disinfectant
physical hazards
poison control center
polish remover
primer
protection
pump
repetitive
safety glasses
skin contact
solvents
vapors
ventilation

Part 2

THE SCIENCE OF NAIL TECHNOLOGY

Nail Product Chemistry Simplified

UNDERSTANDING CHEMICALS

1. Almost everything a nail technician does depends on _____.

2. **Matching.** Match the terms on the left with their correct descriptions on the right.

   _____ 1. molecule   A.   a molecule that cannot be broken down at all

   _____ 2. matter   B.   a change in form or appearance

   _____ 3. chemical change   C.   something that dissolves another substance

   _____ 4. physical change   D.   the force that makes two surfaces stick together

   _____ 5. energy   E.   something that takes up space or occupies an area

   _____ 6. element   F.   one chemical changing into a completely different chemical substance

        G.   a chemical in its simplest form

        H.   light and microwaves are examples of this

3. Under the right conditions, a molecule can chemically change and is called a _____.

4. Vapors are formed when liquids _____ into the air.

5. A chemical that speeds up a chemical reaction is called a _____.

6. A _____ is something that dissolves another substance.

7. The substance that is dissolved is called a _____.

8. The "universal solvent" is _____.

9. The level of solvent should cover the fingers to the bottom of the _____.

10. A chemical that causes two surfaces to stick together is _____.

11. Primers improve adhesion but can be _____ to soft tissue.

12. Moisture can be temporarily removed from the nail with a _____.

13. List five problems related to overfiling.

   a. _____

   b. _____

   c. _____

   d. _____

   e. _____

FINGERNAIL COATINGS

14. List four common nail coatings.

    a. _____

    b. _____

    c. _____

    d. _____

15. **Matching.** Match the terms on the left with their correct descriptions on the right.

    _____ 1. initiator   A. gigantic chains of molecules

    _____ 2. monomer   B. speeds up a chemical reaction

    _____ 3. crosslinker   C. light-cured enhancements need this

    _____ 4. polymer   D. a monomer that joins different polymer chains

    _____ 5. ultraviolet light E. incandescent light

                                                  F. this triggers polymerization

                                                G. individual molecules that join to make a polymer

AVOIDING SKIN PROBLEMS

16. Abnormal skin inflammation is called _____.

17. List two types of contact dermatitis.

    a. _____

    b. _____

18. List four likely places for allergies to occur.

    a. _____

    b. _____

    c. _____

    d. _____

19. Overexposure refers to _____.

20. List four things that cause gels to harden incorrectly, therefore, causing skin problems.

    a. _____

    b. _____

    c. _____

    d. _____

21. Chemicals that enlarge the vessels around an injury site are called _____.

22. Symptoms of contact dermatitis are isolated to _____.

MATCHING REVIEW

Insert the correct word listed in front of each definition below.

adhesive   initiator   polymer
catalyst   matter   solute
contact dermatitis   molecule   solvent
crosslinker   monomer
histamine   overexposure

23. _____ a chemical in its simplest form

24. _____ something that dissolves another substance

25. _____ skin inflammation caused by touching certain substances to the skin

26. _____ a gigantic chain of molecules

27. _____ takes up space or occupies an area

28. _____ chemical that enlarges the vessels around an injury site

29. _____ prolonged, repeated, long-term exposure

30. _____ something that speeds a chemical reaction

31. _____ a monomer that joins polymer chains

32. _____ a chemical that causes two surfaces to stick together

WORD REVIEW

If you do not know the meanings of the words listed below, look them up in the text.

abrasive   dehydrator   molecule
acetone   dermatitis   monomer
adhesion   element   overexposure
adhesive   energy   pigment
alchemist   epidermis   polymer
allergic   evaporate   polymerization
catalyst   flammable   primer
chemical   glue   saturate
chemical change   histamine   sensitization
chemical reaction   incandescent   simple polymer chain
contaminate   incompatible   solute
coatings   initiator   solvent
contact dermatitis   irritant   substance
corrosive   matter   ultraviolet (UV) light
crosslinker   medieval   universal solvent
cyanoacrylate   microwave   volatile

Anatomy and Physiology

INTRODUCTION

1. Explain why a nail technician must study anatomy and physiology.

   _____

   _____

2. List four parts of the human body.

   a. _____

   b. _____

   c. _____

   d. _____

3. Define anatomy.

   _____

4. Define physiology.

   _____

5. Define histology.

   _____

   _____

CELLS

6. Define cells.

   _____

7. **Matching.** Match the terms on the left with their correct descriptions on the right.

   _____ 1. cytoplasm

   _____ 2. cell membrane

   _____ 3. protoplasm

   _____ 4. centrosome

   _____ 5. nucleus

   A. a small round body in the cytoplasm

   B. groups of cells of the same kind

   C. a colorless, jelly-like substance

   D. found in the center of the cell

   E. encloses the cytoplasm

   F. found outside of a cell

   G. found outside the nucleus

   H. a colorful, jelly-like substance

CELL GROWTH

8. Under what five conditions will a cell continue to grow?

   a. _____

   b. _____

   c. _____

   d. _____

   e. _____

9. Cells reproduce themselves through a process of cell division called _____.

10. **Identification.** Using the letters **M**, **A**, and **C** (defined below), match the correct characteristics below.
    Key:
    M = metabolism
    A = anabolism
    C = catabolism
    Characteristics:

    _____ a. stores water, food, and oxygen

    _____ b. complex process where cells are nourished and supplied with energy

    _____ c. breaks down larger molecules into smaller ones

    _____ d. builds up larger molecules from smaller ones

    _____ e. has two phases

    _____ f. releases energy for muscle contraction, secretion, or heat production

11. Define homeostasis.

    _____

12. a. Explain why people gain weight.

    _____

    b. Explain how people can get rid of fat.

    _____

TISSUES

13. Define tissue.

    _____

14. **Matching.** Match the terms on the left with their correct descriptions on the right.

    _____ 1. connective   A. basic unit of all living things

    _____ 2. muscular   B. carries messages to and from the brain

    _____ 3. nerve   C. anabolism and catabolism

    _____ 4. epithelial   D. supports, protects, and binds together other body tissues

    _____ 5. liquid   E. a protective covering on body surfaces

        F. maintains homeostasis

        G. contracts and moves various parts of the body

        H. carries food, waste products, and hormones by means of the blood and lymph

ORGANS

15. Define organs.

    _____

16. **Matching.** Match the terms on the left with their correct descriptions on the right.

    _____ 1. brain   A.   supplies oxygen to the blood

    _____ 2. heart   B.   a storage place for unused fat cells

    _____ 3. lungs   C.   excretes water and other waste products

    _____ 4. kidneys   D.   part of the reproductive system

    _____ 5. stomach   E.   controls the body

                                     F.   digests food

                                     G.   circulates the blood

                                     H.   encloses the protoplasm

                                     I.   removes toxic products of digestion

SYSTEMS

17. a. Define systems.

    _____

    b. How many systems are in the body?

    _____

18. **Matching.** Match the systems on the left with their correct descriptions on the right.

    _____ 1. integumentary   A.   supplies oxygen to the body

    _____ 2. skeletal   B.   produces all the movements of the body

    _____ 3. muscular   C.   made up of duct glands

    _____ 4. nervous   D.   supplies blood throughout the body

    _____ 5. circulatory   E.   the skin's dermis and epidermis

    _____ 6. endocrine   F.   made up of nucleus, centrosome, and cell mem-
                                         brane
    _____ 7. excretory
                                     G.   enables human beings to reproduce
    _____ 8. respiratory
                                     H.   changes food into usable substances
    _____ 9. digestive
                                     I.   the framework of the body
    _____10. reproductive
                                     J.   anabolism and catabolism are part of this system

                                     K.   controls and coordinates the functions of the body
                                          systems

                                     L.   eliminates waste from the body

                                     M.   made up of ductless glands that secrete hormones
                                          into the bloodstream

THE SKELETAL SYSTEM

19. How many bones are on a skeleton?

_____

20. Bone is the _____ tissue of the body, except for tooth enamel.

21. Define osteology.

_____

22. The technical term for bone is _____.

23. List five functions of the skeletal system.

a. _____

b. _____

c. _____

d. _____

e. _____

24. Bone is a hard connective tissue consisting of bone cells called _____.

25. **Matching.** Match the terms on the left with their correct descriptions on the right.

_____ 1. periosteum

_____ 2. cartilage

_____ 3. ligaments

_____ 4. synovial fluid

_____ 5. pivot joint

_____ 6. hinge joint

_____ 7. ball and socket joint

_____ 8. gliding joints

A. two or more bones connect like a door

B. lubricant for the joints

C. another name for collar bone

D. cushions bone at the joints

E. rounded bone fits into the hollow of another bone

F. a fibrous membrane that covers and protects the bone, and aids in bone repair after injury

G. one bone turns on another bone

H. also called osteology

I. two bones glide over each other

J. bands or sheets of fibrous tissue that support bones at the joints

K. technical term for bone

26. Bone receives nutrition from arteries that enter the bone structure through microscopic tunnels called _____.

27. Another name for the collar bone is _____.

28. The fingers, or _____, have three _____ in each finger and two in the thumb.

29. Label the bones of the arm and hand.

1. _____
2. _____
3. _____
4. _____
5. _____
6. _____

1.

4.

2.

5.

3.

6.

30. Label the bones of the leg and foot.

1. _____
2. _____
3. _____
4. _____
5. _____
6. _____
7. _____
8. _____

8.

1.

2.

3.

4.

5.

6.

7.

V IV III II I

31. Similar to the bones of the fingers, the bones of the toes are called _____. There are two of these in the big toe and _____ in the other toes.

THE MUSCULAR SYSTEM

32. Define myology.

_____

33. a. How many muscles are in the body?

_____

   b. What percent of body weight does the muscular system comprise?

_____

34. Define muscles.

_____

35. **Matching**. Match the terms on the left with their correct descriptions on the right.

   _____ 1. striated

   _____ 2. nonstriated

   _____ 3. cardiac

   _____ 4. origin

   _____ 5. insertion

   _____ 6. belly

   _____ 7. massage

   _____ 8. electric current

   _____ 9. light rays

   _____10. heat rays

   _____11. moist heat

   _____12. tendon

   A. muscle part that moves

   B. heart muscle

   C. infrared and ultraviolet are examples

   D. voluntary muscles

   E. also called phalanges

   F. can be performed by hand or electric vibrator

   G. mass of muscle fibers

   H. muscles of the hand

   I. involuntary muscles

   J. also called digits

   K. lamps and caps produce these

   L. applied to muscles to produce visible muscle contractions

   M. muscle part that does not move

   N. example is steam

   O. muscle attached to each end of bone.

36. Explain how pressure is usually directed when massage is performed.

_____

37. **Identification.** Using the letters **A**, **F**, **H**, and **L** (defined below), match the following muscles with the correct part of the body.
   Key:
   A = shoulder and upper arm muscles
   F = forearm muscles
   H = hand muscles
   L = lower leg and foot muscles
   Muscles:

   _____ a. flexor

   _____ b. extensor digitorum longus

   _____ c. extensor

_____ d. adductors

_____ e. biceps

_____ f. peroneus longus

_____ g. gastrocnemius

_____ h. supinator

_____ i. flexor digitorum brevis

_____ j. abductors

_____ k. peroneus brevis

_____ l. deltoid

_____ m. abductor hallucis

_____ n. tibialis anterior

_____ o. pronator

_____ p. opponent

_____ q. triceps

_____ r. soleus

THE NERVOUS SYSTEM

38. Define neurology.

   _____

39. Explain the purpose of the nervous system.

   _____

   _____

40. **Identification.** Using the letters **C**, **P**, and **A** (defined below), match the characteristics below with the three divisions of the nervous system.
   Key:
   C = central nervous system
   P = peripheral nervous system
   A = autonomic nervous system
   Characteristics:

   _____ a. made up of sensory and motor nerve fibers

   _____ b. functions without conscious effort

   _____ c. consists of the brain and spinal cord

   _____ d. has sympathetic and parasympathetic systems

   _____ e. controls the five senses

   _____ f. carries messages to and from the central nervous system

   _____ g. also called the cerebrospinal nervous system

   _____ h. regulates activities of the glands and heart

   _____ i. controls all mental activities

THE BRAIN AND SPINAL CORD

41. The brain is the body's largest mass of _____ tissue and is contained in the
     _____. It weighs _____ ounces.

42. a. Where does the spinal cord originate?

     _____

     b. How many pairs of nerves extend from the spinal cord?

     _____

NERVE CELLS AND NERVES

43. Define nerves.

     _____

     _____

44. **Matching.** Match the terms on the left with their correct descriptions on the right.

     _____ 1. neuron   A.   sends messages to other neurons, glands, or muscles

     _____ 2. dendrites   B.   also called ulnar

     _____ 3. axon   C.   have ability to send and receive messages

     _____ 4. sensory nerves   D.   automatic involuntary response to a stimulus

     _____ 5. motor nerves   E.   also called afferent nerves

     _____ 6. mixed nerves   F.   has sympathetic and parasympathetic systems

     _____ 7. receptors   G.   primary structural unit of the nervous system

     _____ 8. reflex   H.   sensory nerve endings

                                    I.   the body's largest mass of nerve tissue

                                    J.   a cell body that receives messages from other neurons

                                    K.   also called efferent nerves

NERVES OF THE ARM AND HAND

45. Label nerves of the arm and hand.

     1. _____

     2. _____

     3. _____

     4. _____

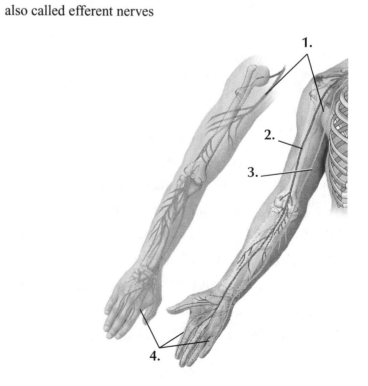

NERVES OF THE LOWER LEG AND FOOT

46. List seven nerves of the lower leg and foot.

    a. _____

    b. _____

    c. _____

    d. _____

    e. _____

    f. _____

    g. _____

THE CIRCULATORY SYSTEM

47. a. What is another name for the circulatory system?

    _____

    b. List two systems within the vascular system.

       1. _____

       2. _____

THE HEART

48. What is the heart?

    _____

49. The heart is enclosed in a membrane called the _____.

50. How many times does the heart beat at the normal resting rate?

    _____

51. List the four chambers of the heart.

    a. _____

    b. _____

    c. _____

    d. _____

52. Tubes that carry blood from the heart are _____ and those that carry blood to the heart are _____.

53. What allows blood to flow in only one direction?

    _____

THE BLOOD

54. Define blood.

    _____

    _____

55. Blood's normal temperature is _____.

56. How many pints of blood are in an adult?

_____

57. Explain why blood changes color from bright to dark red.

_____

_____

58. List two types of blood circulation.

a. _____

b. _____

59. **Matching.** Match the terms on the left with their correct descriptions on the right.

_____ 1. pulmonary circulation   A. carry oxygen to the cells

_____ 2. white corpuscles   B. help the blood to clot

_____ 3. plasma   C. circulation from the heart to the lungs

_____ 4. red corpuscles   D. equalizes body temperature

_____ 5. systemic circulation   E. fluid part of the blood

_____ 6. blood platelets   F. main blood supply to the hand

                                                                   G. circulation from the heart through the body and back to the heart

                                                                    H. tubes that carry blood to the heart

                                                                    I. destroy disease-causing germs

60. List five important functions of the blood.

a. _____

b. _____

c. _____

d. _____

e. _____

61. List six arteries that supply blood to the arms, hands, lower leg, and foot.

a. _____

b. _____

c. _____

d. _____

e. _____

f. _____

THE LYMPH-VASCULAR SYSTEM

62. Define lymph.

_____

63. Explain five functions of lymph.

   a. _____

   b. _____

   c. _____

   d. _____

   e. _____

THE ENDOCRINE SYSTEM

64. Define gland.

   _____

65. What substance(s) do the endocrine glands secrete?

   _____

66. Give three examples of endocrine glands.

   a. _____

   b. _____

   c. _____

THE EXCRETORY SYSTEM

67. Explain how the excretory system purifies the body.

   _____

68. List five body organs that are a part of this system. After each, list the type of waste matter that organ eliminates.

   Organ: Waste Matter:

   1. _____   _____

   2. _____   _____

   3. _____   _____

   4. _____   _____

   5. _____   _____

THE RESPIRATORY SYSTEM

69. a. Spongy tissues composed of microscopic cells that take in air are called _____.

   b. A muscular partition that controls breathing is called the _____.

70. a. The gas we inhale is _____.

   b. The gas we exhale is _____.

THE DIGESTIVE SYSTEM

71. Define digestion.

   _____

72. a. Where does digestion begin?

   _____

b. Where does it end?

_____

c. List three organs between the mouth and small intestine.

    1. _____

    2. _____

    3. _____

73. The large intestine, also called the _____ , stores matter for elimination through the

    _____ .

74. How long does the complete digestive process take?

_____

75. Define digestive enzymes.

_____

_____

76. **Identification.** Using the letters, **S, M, N, C, EN, EX, R,** and **D** (defined below), match the correct characteristics below with one of the body's ten systems.

Key:

S = skeletal system

M = muscular system

N = nervous system

C = circulatory system

EN = endocrine system

EX = excretory system

R = respiratory system

D = digestive system

Characteristics:

_____ a. ductless glands

_____ b. makes up 40% to 50% of body weight

_____ c. cleans the body by eliminating waste

_____ d. supplies oxygen to the body

_____ e. central, peripheral, and autonomic

_____ f. converts food so the body can use it

_____ g. also called the vascular system

_____ h. lungs take in air

_____ i. pharynx, esophagus, and stomach

_____ j. the study of this is osteology

_____ k. urine from the kidneys

_____ l. secretes hormones

_____ m. diaphragm controls breathing

_____ n. bile from the liver

_____ o. origin, belly, and insertion

_____ p. begins in the mouth, ends in the small intestine

_____ q. digits and phalanges

_____ r. glands in it secrete substances

_____ s. the study of this is neurology

_____ t. two types are blood-vascular and lymph-vascular

_____ u. veins, arteries, corpuscles, and lymph-vascular

_____ v. the study of this is myology

_____ w. neurons, sensory, and reflexes

_____ x. joints, periosteum, and ligaments

WORD REVIEW

If you do not know the meanings of the words listed below, look them up in the text.

abductors
abductor hallucis
adductors
afferent nerves
anabolism
anatomy
anterior tibial artery
arteries
auricle
autonomic nervous system
axon and axon terminal
ball-and-socket joint
belly
biceps
blood
blood platelets
blood-vascular system
bones
brain
calcaneous
capillaries
carbon dioxide
cardiac
carpus/wrist
cartilage
catabolism
cell(s)
cell membrane
central nervous system
centrosome
cerebrospinal nervous system
circulatory system
clavicle
common peroneal nerve
connective tissue
cytoplasm
deep peroneal nerve
deltoid

dendrites
diaphragm
digestion
digestive enzymes
digestive system
digital nerve
digits
dorsalis pedis artery
dorsal nerve
ductless glands
efferent nerves
electric current
endocrine system
enzymes
epithelial tissue
erythrocytes
esophagus
excretory system
exhale
extensor
extensor digatorum brevis
extensor digitorum longus
femur
fibula
flexor
flexor digatorum brevis
forearm
gastrocnemius
glands
gliding joints
heart
heat rays
hinge joints
histology
homeostasis
hormones
humerus
inhale

insertion
integumentary system
intestines
joints
kidneys
lacteals
left atrium
left ventricle
leucocytes
ligaments
light rays
liquid tissue
liver
lungs
lymph
lymphatic system
lymph glands
lymph-vascular system
massage
median nerve
metabolism
metacarpals
metatarsals
mitosis
mixed nerves
moist heat
motor nerves
muscular system
muscular tissue
myology
neurology
nerve tissue
nerves
nervous system
neuron
nonstriated
nucleus
opponent

organs
origin
os
osteology
oxygen
parasympathetic system
patella
pericardium
peripheral system
periosteum
peroneus brevis
peroneus longus
perspiration
phalanges
pharynx
physiology
pivot joints
plasma
popliteal artery
posterior tibial artery
pronator
protoplasm

pulmonary circulation
radial artery
radial nerve
radius
receptors
red corpuscles
reflex
reproductive system
respiratory system
right atrium
right ventricle
saphenous nerve
scapula
sensory nerves
sinews
skeletal system
soleus
spinal cord
stomach
striated
superficial peroneal nerve
supinator

sural nerve
sympathetic system
synovial fluid
systemic circulation
systems
tarsal
tendons
tibia
tibial nerve
tibialis anterior
tissues
triceps
ulna
ulnar artery
ulnar nerve
urine
vagus
valves
vascular system
veins
white corpuscles

Date _____

Rating _____

Text Pages 111–129

The Nail and Its Disorders

INTRODUCTION

1. List three characteristics of healthy nails.

   a. _____

   b. _____

   c. _____

2. What is the technical term for nail?

   _____

3. a. Name the protein nails are made of.

   _____

   b. List two other things that are made of the same protein.

   1. _____

   2. _____

4. Explain why we have nails.

   _____

5. a. How fast do fingernails grow?

   _____

   b. The season of the year when nails grow faster is _____.

   c. If a person has lost an entire nail (through disease or accident), how long will it take for the nail to replace itself?

   _____

NORMAL NAIL ANATOMY

6. Label the parts of the nail.

   1. _____

   2. _____

   3. _____

   4. _____

   5. _____

   6. _____

   7. _____

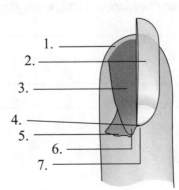

7. **Matching.** Match the nail parts on the left with their correct descriptions on the right.

_____ 1. nail/plate

_____ 2. nail fold

_____ 3. lunula

_____ 4. bed epithelium

_____ 5. keratin

_____ 6. specialized ligaments

_____ 7. free edge

_____ 8. grooves

_____ 9. hyponychium

_____ 10. matrix bed

_____ 11. eponychium

_____ 12. nail bed

_____ 13. cuticle

A. deep folds of skin that surround the nail plate

B. part of the cuticular system

C. skin beneath nail plate/body

D. skin under the free edge

E. atttaches the nail to the nail bed

F. main nail part constructed in layers

G. bottom skin of each toe

H. produces the nail plate

I. nail grows along these tracks

J. crescent of toughened skin around the base of the nail

K. bottom skin of each finger

L. extends beyond the fingertip

M. where nail growth begins

N. nails are made of this protein

O. whitish half-moon shape at nail base

P. anchors the nail bed to the underlying bone

NAIL DISORDERS

8. Define nail disorder.

_____

9. To make a responsible decision about whether you should perform a service on a client, a nail technician must learn to recognize the _____ of nail disorders.

10. List and describe four symptoms of the nail or skin on which a nail technician should not work.

Symptom: Description:

a. _____   _____

b. _____   _____

c. _____   _____

d. _____   _____

11. List the nail plate disorders that can be roughly classified into four individual problem areas.

a. _____

b. _____

c. _____

d. _____

12. **Matching.** Match the terms on the left with their correct descriptions on the right.

_____ 1. furrows or corrugations

_____ 2. onychophagy

_____ 3. discolored nails

_____ 4. onychatrophia or atrophy

_____ 5. pterygium

_____ 6. onychorrhexis

_____ 7. onychocryptosis or ingrown nails

_____ 8. agnails or hangnails

_____ 9. leukonychia

_____ 10. onychauxis or hypertrophy

_____ 11. eggshell nails

_____ 12. melanonychia

A.   split or brittle nails

B.   cuticle is dry, so it splits

C.   fungus infection with blisters

D.   fragile, thin, and curved nails over the free edge

E.   abnormal scarring of the eponychuim or hyponychium.

F.   bitten, deformed nails

G.   long depressions that run lengthwise or across the nail

H.   plate loosens, does not fall or come off

I.   nail appears blue in color

J.   the overgrowth of nails

K.   nail grows into the tissue on the sides of the nail

L.   black band under the nail plate

M.   wasting away of the nail

N.   white spots on the nail

O.   bacterial infection of the tissue around the nail

13. A trumpet or pincer nail can _____ completely in on itself.

14. Plicatured nail figuratively means _____ .

15. Onychgryphosis is called _____ and is the result of injury to the _____ .

16. How can a nail technician correct agnails (hangnails)?

_____

17. List two things that can be applied to hide discolored nails.

a. _____

b. _____

18. Because eggshell nails are fragile and break easily, filing should be done with the _____ side of an emery board. Using a metal pusher at the base of the nail should not be done with much _____ .

19. What type of pusher should be used when manicuring a client who has furrows on her nails?

_____

20. List three causes of leukonychia.

a. _____

b. _____

c. _____

21. Three things that happen to a nail with onychatrophia, or atrophy, are that it loses its
_____ , it _____ , and falls _____ .

22. File an onychauxis or hypertropy nail _____ , and buff it with _____ .

23. If the tissue around the onychocryptosis nail is not infected, you can trim the nail corner in a curved shape to relieve the _____ on the nail groove.

24. Describe how the condition onychophagy can be improved.

_____

25. a. List four causes of onychorrhexis.

    1. _____

    2. _____

    3. _____

    4. _____

    b. List two ways onychorrhexis can be corrected.

    1. _____

    2. _____

26. Explain how pterygium can be treated.

_____

_____

27. a. List eight causes of corrugations.

    1. _____

    2. _____

    3. _____

    4. _____

    5. _____

    6. _____

    7. _____

    8. _____

    b. Discuss how the appearance of corrugations can be corrected if the ridges are not deep and the nail is not broken.

_____

_____

28. **Matching.** Match the terms on the left with their correct descriptions on the right.

_____ 1. onychomycosis (tinea unguium)

_____ 2. onycholysis

_____ 3. pyogenic granuloma

_____ 4. onychia

_____ 5. paronychia

_____ 6. pseudomonas aerugenosa

_____ 7. onychorrhexis

_____ 8. onychomodesis

A. severe inflammation of the soft tissue surrounding the nail in which red tissue grows from the inflamed area.

B. waste from the bacteria turns from yellow-green to black

C. plate lifts from nail bed

D. inflammation of the entire nail unit or part there of

E. white spots on the nail plate

F. split or brittle nails

G. ingrown nails

H. nail-biting

I. an infection of tissue around the nail

J. shedding of the nail plate

K. disease caused by a fungus

29. **Identification.** Using the letters **Y** and **N** (defined below) answer the following question: Can a nail technician perform a service on the following nail disorders?
    Key:
    Y = yes, a service can be performed on this disorder
    N = no, a service cannot be performed on this disorder
    Disorders:

_____ a. leukonychia

_____ b. onychatrophia

_____ c. onychia

_____ d. eggshell nails

_____ e. onychoptosis

_____ f. onychophagy

_____ g. paronychia

_____ h. furrows

_____ i. onychogryposis

_____ j. onychauxis

_____ k. onychocryptosis

_____ l. onycholysis

_____ m. discolored nails

_____ n. pterygium

_____ o. nevus

_____ p. agnails

_____ q. onychorrhexis

_____ r. pyogenic granuloma

26. Below each figure, label the disorder shown.

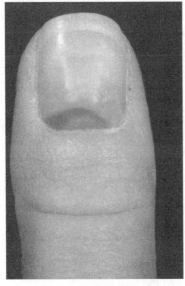

a. _____

_____

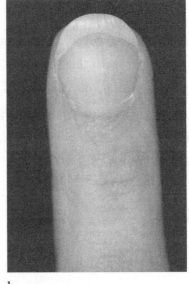

b. _____

_____

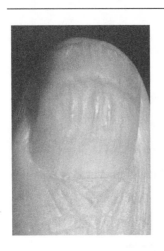

c. _____

_____

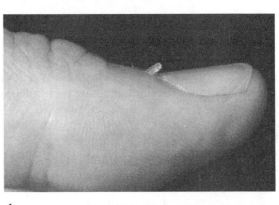

d. _____

_____

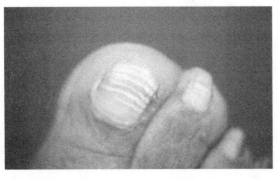

e. _____

_____

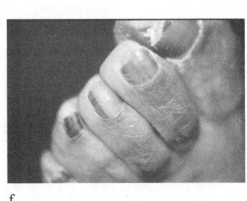

f. _____

_____

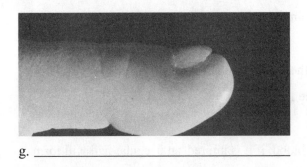

g. _____

_____

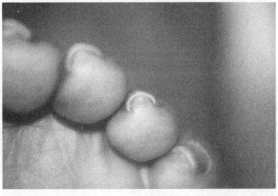

h. _____

_____

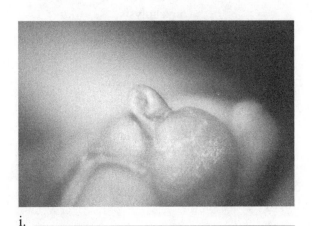

i. _____

_____

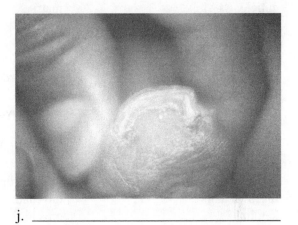

j. _____

_____

MATCHING REVIEW

Insert the correct word listed in front of each definition below.

cuticle   matrix bed   onychophagy
hangnails   nail body/plate   onycholysis
hyponychium   nail root   onyx
keratin   onychia   paronychia
leukonychia   onychocryptosis   pterygium
lunula   onychogryposis

30. _____ technical term for nail

31. _____ cuticle splits because of dryness

32. _____ overlapping skin around the nail

33. _____ where nail growth begins

34. _____ white spots on the nail

35. _____ main nail part constructed in layers

36. _____ nails are made out of this protein

37. _____ nail plate loosens from the nail bed

38. _____ nail-biting

39. _____ half-moon shape at the base of the nail

40. _____ part of skin under the free edge

41. _____ ingrown nails

42. _____ contains nerves and blood; if it is injured, an irregular nail will form

43. _____ an inflammation somewhere in the nail

WORD REVIEW

If you do not know the meanings of the words listed below, look them up in the text.

broken skin	leukonychia	onychocryptosis
bruised nails	lunula	onychogryposis
corrugations	mantle	onychomycosis
cuticle	matrix	onycholysis
dermatologist	mold	onychomadesis
discolored nails	nail bed	onychophagy
eggshell nails	nail body/plate	onychoptosis
eponychium	nail disorder	onychorrhexis
free edge	nail fold	onyx
furrows	nail grooves	paronychia
hangnails (agnails)	nail root	perionychium
hyponychium	nail wall(s)	pterygium
infection	nevus	pyogenic granuloma
inflammation	onychatrophia (atrophy)	raised/swollen skin
ingrown nails	onychauxis (hypertrophy)	
keratin	onychia	

The Skin and Its Disorders

INTRODUCTION

1. Why must a nail technician have a basic understanding of the skin?

   _____

2. Explain two reasons why knowledge of the skin will help you.

   a. _____

   b. _____

HEALTHY SKIN

3. Define dermatology.

   _____

4. List four characteristics of healthy skin.

   a. _____   c. _____

   b. _____   d. _____

5. a. Where is our skin the thickest?   b. Where is our skin the thinnest?

   _____   _____

6. The skin is the _____ of the body.

FUNCTIONS OF THE SKIN

7. **Matching.** Match the terms on the left with their correct descriptions on the right.

   _____ 1. protection

   _____ 2. secretion

   _____ 3. absorption

   _____ 4. prevention of fluid loss

   _____ 5. respiration

   _____ 6. heat regulation

   _____ 7. excretion

   _____ 8. response to external stimuli

   A. skin seals blood and other fluids inside the body

   B. sudoriferous gland records hot, cold, pain, and pleasure

   C. maintain 98.6° F

   D. skin's shield from injury and bacteria invasion

   E. oxygen taken in and carbon dioxide is discharged

   F. pores take in small amounts of chemicals, drugs, and cosmetics

   G. sebum eliminates wastes

   H. skin's sensitivity to heat, cold, touch, pressure, and pain

   I. carbon dioxide taken in and oxygen is discharged

   J. perspiration removes salt and other wastes

STRUCTURE OF THE SKIN

8. Label the microscopic section of the skin.

    1. _____

    2. _____

    3. _____

    4. _____

    5. _____

    6. _____

    7. _____

9. **Identification.** Using the letters **E** and **D** (defined below), match the characteristics below with one of the skin layers.

    Key:

    E = epidermis

    D = dermis

    Characteristics:

    _____ 1. contains two separate layers

    _____ 2. blood vessels, nerves, sweat, and oil glands are found in this layer

    _____ 3. also called cuticle

    _____ 4. made up of four layers called stratums

    _____ 5. deep layer of the skin

    _____ 6. papillary, reticular, and subcutaneous

    _____ 7. melanin is found here

    _____ 8. contains nerve endings but no blood vessels

    _____ 9. adipose tissue is found here

    _____ 10. outer layer of the skin

    _____ 11. also called true skin, corium, or cutis

    _____ 12. keratinized cells are found here

10. List four layers of the epidermis.

    a. _____

    b. _____

    c. _____

    d. _____

11. a. The name of the skin coloring pigment is _____.

    b. The special cells that make the skin coloring pigment are found in the stratum

    _____ .

    c. The skin coloring pigment protects the body from the destructive effects of _____ rays.

12. a. List the layers of the dermis.

    1. _____

    2. _____

b. Which layer of the dermis is directly below the epidermis?

_____

13. a. Which layer under the dermis is made up of fatty tissue?

_____

b. Another name for the fatty tissue is _____.

c. Explain three purposes or functions of this fatty tissue.

1. _____

2. _____

3. _____

NOURISHMENT OF THE SKIN

14. What is lymph?

_____

15. List three parts of a network through which blood and lymph circulate through the skin.

a. _____

b. _____

c. _____

16. For what three things do the blood and lymph supply growth and repair nourishment?

a. _____

b. _____

c. _____

NERVES OF THE SKIN

17. Explain the action(s) of nerves.

_____

_____

18. a. List three types of nerves.

1. _____

2. _____

3. _____

b. Which type of nerve causes goose bumps?

_____

c. The nerves of the sweat and oil glands are called _____ nerves.

d. Which type of nerve reacts to touch?

_____

GLANDS OF THE SKIN

19. a. The skin contains two types of _____ glands.

b. Explain what duct glands do to materials from the blood.

_____

c. List two actions that may happen to these different materials from the blood.

1. _____

2. _____

19. **Identification.** Using the letters **SU** and **SE** (defined below), match the correct characteristics below with one type of gland.
   Key:
   SU = sudoriferous gland
   SE = sebaceous gland
   Characteristics:

   _____ a. eliminates one to two pints of liquid daily

   _____ b. not found on the palms or soles

   _____ c. regulates body temperature

   _____ d. also called oil glands

   _____ e. lubricates skin and softens hair

   _____ f. palms, soles, forehead, and armpits have the greatest number of them

   _____ g. a blackhead may form

   _____ h. also called sweat glands

   _____ i. has a coiled base called a fundus

   _____ j. opens into the hair follicle

   _____ k. secretes sebum

   _____ l. eliminates waste

ELASTICITY OF THE SKIN

21. a. Explain the action of the elastic tissue in the papillary layer.

   _____

   b. The elastic tissue is composed of _____.

22. Why does skin sag or wrinkle?

   _____

SKIN DISORDERS

23. Explain why nail technicians need to learn about skin disorders.

   _____

   _____

24. The only person qualified to diagnose a disorder/disease is a _____.

25. List four skin signs that indicate disease is present.

   a. _____

   b. _____

   c. _____

   d. _____

26. Define lesion.

_____

_____

27. Label the skin lesions shown in each diagram.

28. Describe the following lesions.

a. cyst _____

_____

b. macule _____

_____

c. papule _____

_____

d. pustule _____

_____

e. tubercle _____

_____

f. tumor _____

_____

29. **Matching.** Match the terms on the left with their correct descriptions on the right.

_____ 1. excoriation

_____ 2. scales

_____ 3. vesicle

_____ 4. crust

_____ 5. stain

_____ 6. ulcer

_____ 7. fissure

_____ 8. bulla

_____ 9. wheals (hives)

_____10. scar

A. bug bites or allergic reactions cause these

B. example is severe dandruff

C. an open lesion on the skin

D. a scab on a sore, for example

E. a light colored raised mark formed after an injury has healed

F. fluid lump above and below the skin's surface

G. poison ivy produces these small blisters

H. abnormal cell mass that varies in size, shape, and color

I. large blister with watery fluid

J. a sore or abrasion caused by scratching or scraping the superficial layer of the skin

K. discoloration remains after moles, freckles, or liver spots have disappeared

L. chapped hands or lips are examples

M. small pimple that does not contain fluid

INFLAMMATORY AND INFECTIOUS DISORDERS OF THE SKIN

30. Another name for skin inflammation is _____.

31. a. List two skin inflammations.

　　1. _____

　　2. _____

b. Which skin inflammation has silvery plaque-like lesions?

_____

c. Which skin inflammation itches, burns, and has oozing blisters?

_____

d. Which skin inflammation can cause Beau's Lines?

_____

32. a. Localized reactions of the skin to friction from an external source are called _____.

b. They are filled with a _____.

c. It is best not to _____ the blister but to let it _____.

33. List four other causes of blisters.

a. _____

b. _____

c. _____

d. _____

34. a. Calluses are the result of _____ on the skin.

    b. Calluses are formed by the skin to protect itself from _____ .

    c. The yellow discoloration of the callus is due to the _____ within the tissue.

35. List three common names for warts.

    a. _____

    b. _____

    c. _____

FUNGAL INFECTIONS, PIGMENTATION, HYPERTROPIES OF THE SKIN

36. Describe two factors that determine the skin's color.

    a. _____

    b. _____

37. Define hypertropies.

    _____

38. Name two classifications of fungi.

    a. _____

    b. _____

39. The word tinea comes from the Latin word for _____ .

40. Tinea pedis is another term for _____ .

41. Fungi form _____ that have a hard outer coating like an _____ .

42. Worm-like appearance of the advancing edges of an infection is called _____ .

43. a. List two types of fungal infections.

        1. _____

        2. _____

    b. Which fungal infection has blisters?

        _____

    c. Which fungal infection can cause deep cuts to the toes?

        _____

    d. Which fungal infection has a dry scaly formation on the skin?

        _____

44. An acute inflammatory form of fungus, with cuts between the toes and known as _____ , should not be serviced by the nail technician.

45. a. A _____ is the most common _____ of the skin.

    b. Name five things that happen to moles as they mature.

        1. _____

        2. _____

        3. _____

        4. _____

        5. _____

c. If the nevus changes in _____ or _____ , advise the client to seek a _____ .

46. Define melanoma.

_____

47. A complete cure of this disease depends on _____ and _____ .

48. Define herpes simplex.

_____

49. **Matching.** Match the terms on the left with their correct descriptions on the right.

_____ 1. leucoderma   A. freckles

_____ 2. vitiligo   B. general term for abnormal lack of pigmentation

_____ 3. lentigines   C. ultraviolet rays cause this skin darkening

_____ 4. chloasma   D. congenital absence of melanin

_____ 5. herpes simplex E. skin cancer

_____ 6. albinism   F. Tinea pedis fungal infection

_____ 7. tan   G. a blackhead

_____ 8. melanoma   H. acquired form of leucoderma that affects skin or hair

_____ 9. athlete's foot

_____10. mole   I. liver spots

                             J. viral infection

                             K. a wart

                             L. inflammatory skin condition with oozing blisters

                             M. small brown spot on the skin

                             N. red lesions occurring in patches or rings over the hands

MATCHING REVIEW

Insert the correct word listed in front of each definition below.

albininism   hypertropies   scale
dermatology   lesion   sebaceous
dermis   lymph   secretory
epidermis   macule   sensory
fissure   melanin   sudoriferous
heat regulation   nevus

50. _____ outer layer of the skin

51. _____ nerves of the sweat and oil glands

52. _____ study of healthy skin and skin disorders

53. _____ slightly yellow, watery fluid in the body

54. _____ also called sweat glands

55. _____ name of the skin coloring pigment

56. _____ examples are chapped hands or lips

57. _____ keeping the temperature at 98.6° F

58. _____ structural change in tissue caused by injury and disease

59. _____ also called the true skin or corium

60. _____ small, discolored spot or patch on the skin's surface

61. _____ also called oil gland

62. _____ example is severe dandruff

63. _____ new growths

WORD REVIEW

If you do not know the meanings of the words listed below, look them up in the text.

absorption	external stimulus	respiration
adipose tissue	fissure	reticular layer
albinism	freckles	ringworm of the foot
arrector pili	fundus	ringworm of the hand
athlete's foot	heat regulation	scales
basal layer	herpes simplex	scar
blackhead	horny layer	scarf skin
blood	hypertropies	sebaceous glands
broken skin	infected skin	sebum
bulla	inflamed skin	secretory nerves
callus	keratoma	secretion
carbon dioxide	lentigines	sensory nerves
chloasma	lesions	stain
comedone	leucoderma	stratum corneum
complex sensations	lymph	stratum germinativum
corium	macule	stratum granulosum
corn	Malpighian layer	stratum lucidum
crust	melanin	stratum mucosum
cuticle	melanoma sarcoma	subcutaneous tissue
cutis	mole	sudoriferous glands
cyst	motor nerves	sweat glands
derma	nevus	sweat pore
dermatitis	nerve	tactile corpuscle
dermatology	nodule	tan
dermis	oil glands	tinea pedis
duct glands	oxygen	tumor
eczema	papillary layer	tubercle
elastic tissue	papule	ulcer
elasticity	protection	vesicle
epidermis	psoriasis	vitiligo
excoriation	pustule	wheals (hives)
excretion	raised skin	

Date _____

Rating _____

Text Pages 151–160

Client Consultation

COMPLETION

1. Define client consultation.

   _____

2. During the consultation, you will choose the _____ best suited for the client and you
   will complete an evaluation about the _____ of the client's nails.

3. List the two parts of the client consultation.

   a. _____

   b. _____

4. List four ways you can make a good impression during the consultation.

   a. _____

   b. _____

   c. _____

   d. _____

5. List four things you would see if the client has a nail or skin disorder.

   a. _____

   b. _____

   c. _____

   d. _____

6. a. If you need to refer a client to a physician, you must act _____ and

      _____.

   b. To avoid causing unnecessary stress for your client, never attempt to _____ a
      problem or disorder.

7. If a client has an allergic reaction to a product, note on the client _____ which specific
   _____ caused the reaction.

8. The client has asked for a specific service. List two further questions you need to ask in relation to
   this service.

   a. _____

   b. _____

9. Does the client always know which service is the best one for him? Explain why or why not in
   detail.

   _____

_____

_____

_____

10. Listed below are four different lifestyles or hobbies people have. Next to each one, list the types of nail care these people may require.

    a. gardener   _____

    b. guitar player _____

                       _____

    c. model   _____

    d. runner   _____

11. Performing the wrong service on a client could make that person unhappy and even cause _____ . If the client is not happy with the service, you will _____ a client.

12. a. After talking with the client about her needs, expectations, and health, you will either _____ the client's service choice or recommend _____ .

    b. Keep your client's _____ in mind at all times.

COMPLETION REVIEW

Insert the correct word listed in the sentences below.

client record	disorder	product
client consultation	health	service
diagnose	open sores	tactfully

13. If you see inflammation, infection, redness, or _____ , it means that the client has a nail or skin _____ .

14. A meeting where you discuss the client's desires, needs, and nail health is called a/an _____ .

15. If a client has an allergic reaction to a product, note it on the client _____ .

16. During the consultation, you will choose the best suited _____ for the client.

17. If you need to refer a client to a physician, you must act responsibly and _____ .

WORD REVIEW

If you do not know the meanings of the words listed below, look them up in the text.

allergic reaction	disorders	job
appropriate	evaluation	lifestyle
client record	examine	nail health
client consultation	expectations	open skin
client desires	explain	recommend
client needs	hobbies	redness
decision	infection	result
diagnose	inflammation	safety

Part 3

BASIC PROCEDURES

10

Manicuring

EQUIPMENT

1. Manicuring equipment are _____ items and only when they wear out do they have to be _____ .

2. **Matching.** Match the terms on the left with their correct descriptions on the right.

   _____ 1. disinfection container

   _____ 2. lactel heater

   _____ 3. supply tray

   _____ 4. client's cushion

   _____ 5. manicure table

   _____ 6. electric nail dryer

   _____ 7. cotton container

   _____ 8. fingerbowl

   A. used to trim away excess cuticle at the nail's base

   B. shaped for soaking the client's fingers

   C. shortens the nail drying time

   D. holds a disinfectant solution in which to immerse objects to be sanitized

   E. holds absorbent cotton or lint-free wipes

   F. also called a cuticle pusher

   G. most include a drawer to store sanitized implements

   H. adds shine to the nail plate

   I. holds polishes, polish removers, and creams

   J. can be either 8" x 12" or a folded towel

   K. warms lotion for a hot oil manicure

IMPLEMENTS

3. After using a manicuring implement on a client, the implement or tool must either be _____ or _____ .

4. What size are manicuring implements?

   _____

5. **Identification.** Using the letters **OS, MF, EB, CN, NB,** and **CB** (defined below), match the correct characteristics below with one manicuring implement.
   Key:
   OS = orangewood stick
   MF = metal nail file
   EB = emery board
   CN = cuticle nipper
   NB = nail brush
   CB = chamois buffer
   Characteristics:

   _____ 1. used to shape the free edge of hard nails

_____ 2. used to file soft or fragile nails

_____ 3. hold it so the blades face the cuticle

_____ 4. loosens the cuticle around the nail's base

_____ 5. adds shine to the nail

_____ 6. used to shape the free edge of sculptured nails

_____ 7. smooths out wavy ridges on the nails

_____ 8. remove bits of cuticle with warm soapy water

_____ 9. has a coarse and a fine side

_____10. used to clean under the free edge

_____11. used to trim away excess cuticle

_____12. cleans the fingernails

6. a. A steel pusher is also called a/an _____. It is used to push back excess cuticle
    _____.

    b. The spoon end of a steel pusher is used to _____ and _____ cuticle.

7. Which implement can be used to lift small bits of cuticle from the nail?

    _____

8. Name two implements that must be discarded if they are dropped on the floor.

    a. _____

    b. _____

9. How often must a metal nail file be disinfected?

    _____

10. a. List two types of chamois buffers.

    1. _____

    2. _____

    b. How often must a chamois be changed?

    _____

11. If your client's nails are very long, which implement can be used to shorten the filing time?

    _____

12. List the procedure for sanitizing implements.

    a. _____

    b. _____

    c. _____

    d. _____

    e. _____

13. Identify the parts, tools, and so forth on a manicuring table.

1. _____
2. _____
3. _____
4. _____
5. _____
6. _____
7. _____
8. _____

14. What is the usual soaking time for implements to be in a disinfection container?

_____

15. Why is it necessary to have two sets of metal implements?

_____

_____

MATERIALS

16. How often do manicuring materials need to be replaced? _____

17. **Matching.** Match the terms on the left with their correct descriptions on the right.

_____ 1. plastic spatula   A. used to dry client's hand

_____ 2. alum   B. shapes the nail's free edge

_____ 3. plastic bags   C. used to stop bleeding

_____ 4. towels   D. used to remove nail cosmetics from their containers

_____ 5. cotton   E. used to soak client's hands

                         F. holds discarded materials

                         G. wrapped on the end of an orangewood stick

18. Why are styptic pencils not used in most states?

_____

NAIL COSMETICS

19. **Matching.** Match the terms on the left with their correct descriptions on the right.

_____ 1. base coat

_____ 2. cuticle cream

_____ 3. cuticle oil

_____ 4. nail bleach

_____ 5. hand cream

_____ 6. liquid soap

_____ 7. top coat

_____ 8. colored polish, liquid enamel, or lacquer

_____ 9. nail strengthener/ hardener

_____ 10. cuticle remover/ solvent

_____ 11. nail whitener

_____ 12. polish remover

_____ 13. liquid nail dry

_____ 14. dry nail polish or pumice powder

A. adds color to the nails; contains solution of nitrocellulose in a volatile solvent such as amyl acetate

B. used with warm water in a fingerbowl

C. keeps cuticle soft; contains vegetable oil, vitamin E, mineral oil, jojoba, or palm nut oil

D. used to cut excess cuticle from the nails

E. applied under the free edge to make the nail appear white; contains zinc oxide or titanium dioxide

F. used with a chamois buffer to add shine; contains mild abrasives

G. removes nail polish; contains organic solvents and acetone

H. softens and smooths the hands; contains emollients and humectants such as glycerin, cocoa butter, lecithin, and gums

I. contains 2% to 5% sodium or potassium hydroxide plus glycerin; makes cuticles easier to remove and minimizes clipping

J. promotes rapid polish drying; contains alcohol base

K. applied to the bare nail before polish; contains ethyl acetate, a solvent, isopropyl alcohol, butyl acetate, nitrocellulose, and sometimes formaldehyde

L. used to sanitize the manicure table

M. lubricates and softens dry cuticles and brittle nails

N. bowl used to soak fingers

O. applied over colored polish to prevent chipping; could contains acrylic or cellulose type film formers

P. removes yellow stains from the nail; contains hydrogen peroxide

Q. prevents splitting and peeling of the nail; can contain collagen, nylon fibers, or formaldehyde

20. List four forms of soap.

a. _____

b. _____

c. _____

d. _____

21. a. List two ingredients found in polish remover.

1. _____

2. _____

b. The type of polish remover to use on clients who have artificial nails is

_____

22. a. What ingredient is in nail bleach?

    _____

    b. If nail bleach gets on the skin, it may cause _____.

23. Why are nail white pencils not permitted in most states?

    _____

24. List two forms of dry nail polish.

    a. _____

    b. _____

25. Describe two purposes of a base coat.

    a. _____

    b. _____

26. List three types of nail strengtheners.

    a. _____

    b. _____

    c. _____

27. a. What is the base of a liquid nail dry? _____

    b. List two forms of liquid nail dry.

       1. _____

       2. _____

28. Which has a thicker consistency, hand cream or hand lotion?

    _____

PROCEDURE FOR BASIC TABLE SET-UP

29. When setting up for a manicure, the table should be sanitized with a/an _____.

30. A client's arm cushion should be wrapped in a _____.

31. a. What goes into a disinfection container before putting your implements in it?

    _____

    b. Which manicuring implements are to be placed in the disinfection container?

    _____

32. If the manicurist is left-handed, on which side of the table is a plastic bag to be attached?

    _____

33. List five items that can be kept in the table drawer.

    a. _____

    b. _____

c. _____

d. _____

e. _____

PREPARING CLIENT FOR A MANICURE

34. List five nail shapes.

    a. _____

    b. _____

    c. _____

    d. _____

    e. _____

35. Which nail shape is the most common choice for male clients?

    _____

36. Which nail shape is well suited for thin hands?

    _____

37. Describe four considerations when deciding what nail shape is best for the client.

    a. _____

    b. _____

    c. _____

    d. _____

38. Describe the seven steps to be completed if blood becomes visible during a manicure.

    a. _____

    b. _____

    c. _____

    d. _____

    e. _____

    f. _____

    g. _____

PROCEDURE FOR PLAIN MANICURE

39. Name the three-part sequence of a manicure service.

    a. _____

    b. _____

    c. _____

40. a. If the client is right-handed, with which of their hands do you begin a manicure?

    _____

    b. If the client is left-handed, with which of their hands do you begin a manicure?

    _____

    c. Why do you begin working on the hand that you do?

    _____

41. List the steps for a plain manicure. Assume you are manicuring only one hand. Some steps are written for you.

a.   <u>Remove polish.</u>

b.   <u>Shape the nails.</u>

c. _____

d. _____

e. _____

f. _____

g. _____

h. _____

i. _____

j.   <u>Optional: Bleach nails.</u>

k. _____

l. _____

m._____

n. _____

o. _____

p. _____

q.   <u>Apply polish.</u>

42. To remove polish from the cuticle area, it may be necessary to put cotton on the tip of a/an _____ .

43. a. Nails are to be filed from corner to _____ .

b. Explain why you shape the nails before soaking them.

_____

_____

44. If too much pressure is used when pushing the cuticle back at the base of the nail, it could cause damage to the _____ .

45. When nipping cuticles, be careful not to cut into the mantle because this will _____ .

46. What is the buffing pattern on the nails when using a chamois buffer?

_____

47. List four coats of nail polish that are to be applied to the client's nails.

a. _____

b. _____

c. _____

d. _____

48. Polish corrector pens should not be used because of _____ .

49. Identify the five types of polished nails:

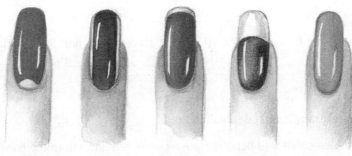

_____   _____   _____   _____   _____

50. List six plain manicure post-service procedures.

a. _____

b. _____

c. _____

d. _____

e. _____

f. _____

FRENCH MANICURE

51. List four steps of a French manicure.

a. _____

b. _____

c. _____

d. _____

RECONDITIONING MANICURE

52. List three items needed to perform a reconditioning manicure.

a. _____

b. _____

c. _____

53. What is done in a reconditioning manicure that is not done in a plain manicure?

_____

ELECTRIC FILE MANICURE

54. a. List three electric file attachments.

1. _____

2. _____

3. _____

b. Using the three attachments you listed in question 54a, complete the following sentences (assume a plain manicure).

1. A chamois buffer works like the _____ attachment.

2. An emery board is most like the _____ attachment.

3. A round abrasive is like the _____ attachment.

55. Holding any attachment for the electric file in one place on the nail for an extended about of time can cause a/an _____ sensation or _____ the nail.

PARAFFIN WAX

56. A paraffin treatment traps heat and moisture, and _____ .

57. List two types of clients that will benefit from a paraffin treatment to the hands and feet.

    a. _____

    b. _____

58. How many times is the hand or foot dipped in paraffin?

    _____

59. How long is paraffin left on the hand or foot?

    _____

HAND AND ARM MASSAGE

60. List two things a massage does for the client.

    a. _____

    b. _____

61. In hand massage, the relaxer movement is also known as the _____ movement.

62. A light stroking massage movement that relaxes and soothes is called _____ .

63. A wringing movement on the arm is also known as a/an _____ type of massage movement.

64. Kneading the arm is also called the _____ movement. It is very stimulating and _____ blood flow.

65. Rotating the client's elbow is a type of massage movement known as _____ .

SPA MANICURES

66. Spa manicures are more _____ than a plain manicure.

67. What two things should all spa manicures include?

    a. _____

    b. _____

MATCHING REVIEW

Insert the correct word listed in front of each definition below.

alcohol	client's cushion	fingerbowl
alum	cuticle nipper	French manicure
approved hospital-grade disinfectant	effleurage	hydrogen peroxide
	electric file	left hand
base coat	electric nail dryer	nail bleach
chamois buffer	emery board	nail strengthener

| nail whitener | petrissage | styptic pencil |
| orangewood stick | right hand | supply tray |

68. _____ has a coarse and a fine side

69. _____ on a right-handed person, begin with this

70. _____ a light stroking massage movement

71. _____ holds polishes, removers, and creams

72. _____ smooths out ridges and adds nail shine

73. _____ removes yellow stains from the nail

74. _____ shortens nail drying time

75. _____ prevents nail splitting and chipping

76. _____ used to trim away ragged cuticle or hangnails

77. _____ an ingredient in nail bleach

78. _____ either an 8" x 12" cushion or a folded towel

79. _____ applied to the bare nail before polish

80. _____ used to stop bleeding

81. _____ base ingredient of liquid nail dry

82. _____ used to clean under the free edge

83. _____ emery disk, cuticle pusher, cuticle brush, and buffer attachments

84. _____ an implement disinfectant grade disinfectant)

85. _____ a kneading massage movement

86. _____ shaped for soaking the client's fingers

87. _____ applied under the free edge to make the nail appear white

WORD REVIEW

If you do not know the meanings of the words listed below, look them up in the text.

abrasives
acetone
adjustable lamp
base coat
bevel
chamois buffer
client chair
client's cushion
colored polish
cotton
cotton balls
cotton plegets
cuticle cream
cuticle nipper
cuticle oil
cuticle solvent or remover
disinfection container
disposable towels

dry nail polish
effleurage massage movement
electric file
electric manicure
electric nail dryer
emery board
equipment
fingerbowl
fingernail clippers
free edge polish application
French manicure
friction massage movement
full coverage polish application
hairline tip polish application
half-moon or lunula polish
   application
hand cream
hand lotion

hospital-grade disinfectant
hot oil
hot oil heater
implements
joint massage movement
kneading massage movement
liquid enamel
liquid nail dry
liquid soap
manicure table
materials
metal nail file
nail bleach
nail brush
nail cosmetics
nail lacquer
nail strengthener or hardener
nail technician's chair or stool

nail whitener
nonacetone
orangewood stick
oval nail
paraffin
petrissage massage movement
plain manicure
plastic bags
plastic spatula

pointed nail
polish remover
powdered alum
reconditioning manicure
relaxer massage movement
round nail
sanitized cotton container
slim line or free-walls polish
    application

square nail
squoval nail
steel pusher
styptic powder
supply tray
terry towels
top coat
tweezers

11

Pedicuring

INTRODUCTION

1. List four things included in a pedicure procedure.

   a. _____

   b. _____

   c. _____

   d. _____

2. Describe two improvements pedicures provide for a client.

   a. _____

   b. _____

3. a. What type of shoes should a client wear to the salon for her pedicure appointment?

   _____

   b. Why this type of shoe?

   _____

PEDICURE EQUIPMENT AND MATERIALS

4. **Matching.** Match the terms on the left with their correct descriptions on the right.

   _____ 1. foot bath   A. keeps toes apart

   _____ 2. toenail clippers   B. disposable paper or foam

   _____ 3. pedicuring stool   C. should have an arm rest and be comfortable

   _____ 4. foot file   D. loosens the nail's cuticle

   _____ 5. foot powder   E. shortens the length of the toenails

   _____ 6. toe separators   F. disposable paper foot slippers

   _____ 7. pedicuring station   G. keeps feet dry after a pedicure

   _____ 8. foot lotion   H. filled with warm soapy water

   _____ 9. client's chair   I. includes two chairs and a foot rest

   _____ 10. pedicure slippers   J. used during a foot massage

        K. nail technician's low stool

        L. removes ingrown toenails

        M. removes dry skin or callus growth

PEDICURE PRESERVICE PROCEDURE

5. List three items that are part of a pedicure station setup.

   a. _____

   b. _____

   c. _____

6. List two places where you should put towels in preparation for a pedicure.

   a. _____

   b. _____

7. Besides standard manicuring implements, list eight additional items for a pedicure.

   a. _____

   b. _____

   c. _____

   d. _____

   e. _____

   f. _____

   g. _____

   h. _____

8. Add _____ to the foot bath.

9. What do you do if you notice an infection or inflammation on your client's feet?

   _____

PEDICURE PROCEDURE

10. List the steps for a pedicure procedure. Assume you are performing a pedicure on one foot. Some steps are written for you.

   a. __Remove shoes and socks._____

   b. _____

   c. _____

   d. _____

   e. _____

   f. _____

   g. _____

   h. _____

   i _____

   j. __Use foot file._____

   k. _____

   l. _____

   m. _____

   n. __Push cuticle back._____

o. _____

p. _____

q. _____

r. _____

s. _____

t. __Powder feet._____

11. Client's feet should soak in a soap bath for at least _____ minutes.

12. In what shape should toenails be filed?

_____

13. List four coats of nail polish that are included in a pedicure service.

a. _____

b. _____

c. _____

d. _____

PEDICURE POSTSERVICE PROCEDURE

14. List six steps of a pedicure post-service procedure.

a. _____

b. _____

c. _____

d. _____

e. _____

f. _____

15. List three pedicure items that are to be wiped with hospital-grade disinfectant after using.

a. _____

b. _____

c. _____

FOOT MASSAGE

16. List three client medical conditions that could preclude receiving a foot massage.

a. _____

b. _____

c. _____

17. The relaxing massage movement is called _____.

18. List three parts of the foot where this relaxing massage movement is performed.

a _____

b. _____

c. _____

19. Deep rubbing movements, such as the thumb and fist twist compression, are also known as _____ massage movements.

20. What is another name for a kneading massage movement?

    _____

21. List two names used for a light tapping movement over the foot.

    a. _____

    b. _____

22. During a foot massage, a plantar's wart should not have _____ applied to that area.

23. List three classes of pedicure products.

    a. _____

    b. _____

    c. _____

24. Therapeutic skin softeners give the feet a special _____ experience.

25. Hot paraffin baths _____ and help reduce _____.

26. List three health reasons a client should not receive a paraffin bath.

    a. _____

    b. _____

    c. _____

27. List six implements that can be invaluable during a pedicure.

    a. _____

    b. _____

    c. _____

    d. _____

    e. _____

    f. _____

28. Toenail nippers can have either _____ or _____ jaws.

29. A curette is a small _____ -shaped instrument.

30. A nail rasp is constructed so that it only files in _____ direction.

31. A major advantage of the diamond nail file is that it is easily _____.

MATCHING REVIEW

Insert the correct word/term listed in front of each definition below.

closed-toe	friction	straight across
curved	nail rasp	tapotement
effleurage	open-toed	toenail clippers
foot bath	pedicure	toe separators
foot file	pedicuring stool	
foot powder	petrissage	

32. _____ shortens the length of the toenails

33. _____ relaxing massage movement

34. _____ includes trimming, shaping, massage, and polishing the toenails

35. _____ removes dry skin or callus growth

36. _____ kneading massage movement

37. _____ shape or direction into which toenails should be filed

38. _____ type of shoes client should wear for a pedicure appointment

39. _____ keeps toes apart during a pedicure

40. _____ a light, tapping massage movement

41. _____ filled with warm soapy water

42. _____ deep rubbing massage movements such as thumb and fist twist compression

43. _____ keeps feet dry after a pedicure

44. _____ cuts or files in one direction

WORD REVIEW

If you do not know the meanings of the words listed below, look them up in the text.

antiseptic, antifungal foot spray

callus

client's chair

curette

effleurage

fist twist massage movement

foot bath or basin

foot file

foot lotion

foot powder

foot rest

friction

ingrown toenails

liquid soap

massage movement

metatarsal scissors

nail rasp

pedicure

pedicure slippers

pedicure station

pedicure stool

percussion

petrissage

plantar's wart

relaxer massage movement

tapotement

thumb compression massage movement

toe separators

toenail clippers

toenail nippers

12

Electric Filing

INTRODUCTION

1. What are electric files?

   _____

2. What do the letters AEFM stand for?

   _____

3. How are "rings of fire" created?

   _____

4. Give two causes of heat when using the electric file.

   a. _____

   b. _____

5. Complete this sentence. Practice makes _____ in overcoming your

   _____ .

6. List two ways in which you can improve your confidence when working with the electric file.

   a. _____

   b. _____

7. Name five types of electric files.

   a. _____

   b. _____

   c. _____

   d. _____

   e. _____

8. Which of these files are not widely used in the nail industry?

   a. _____

   b. _____

CHOOSING AN ELECTRIC FILE

9. Why does the casing on the machine and hand piece have to be sealed tight?

   _____

10. What two things help determine which machine is right for you?

    a. _____

    b. _____

11. What do the letters RPM stand for?

    _____

12. What does RPM mean?

    _____

13. Define torque.

    _____

14. When you bear down on the bit while it's in use, the torque will _____ .

15. List three ways a foot pedal can help you.

    a. _____

    b. _____

    c. _____

16. List two reasons that determine how long an electric file will last.

    a. _____

    b. _____

17. How often should your file be cleaned?

    _____

BITS

18. What is another term for bit?

    _____

19. The industry standard for shank size is _____ .

20. List the two kinds of bits you can buy.

    a. _____

    b. _____

21. When bits are perfectly balanced and the spin exactly centered, they are said to be _____ .

22. a. If 100 grits cover one square inch, the file bit is _____ .

    b. If 240 grits cover one square inch, the file bit is _____ .

23. Carbide bits are measured by the cuts in each bit called _____ .

24. a. The larger and deeper the cuts, the _____ the bit.

    b. The smaller and shallower the cuts, the _____ the bit.

TYPES OF BITS USED ON THE NAIL

25. **Matching.** Match the bit on the left with its correct description on the right.

_____ 1. natural nail bit	A. made of metal with flutes
_____ 2. sanding bit	B. made to trench out growth at smile line
_____ 3. diamond bit	C. long and slender for drilling a hole
_____ 4. carbide bit	D. round paper files used on a mandrel
_____ 5. backfill	E. for use on callus
_____ 6. buffing	F. ceramic stone, barrel-shaped
_____ 7. abrasive stone	G. chamois, leather, or cotton ragwheels
_____ 8. pedicure bit	H. have diamond particles attached with adhesive
_____ 9. jewelry bit	I. synthetic rubber can smooth out ridges

26. Proper procedures of _____ and disinfection should be used on the bits.

27. List two reasons bits can rust.

    a. _____

    b. _____

28. Always keep the bit _____ while in use.

29. Graduating grits is the key to _____.

MATCHING REVIEW

Insert the correct word/term listed in front of each definition below.

AEFM	flutes	RPMs
backfill bit	grit	rings of fire
bits	jewelry bit	torque
concentric	maintenance	

30. _____ used to bevel a trench for filling of the smile line

31. _____ horsepower

32. _____ educates nationally and establishes standards

33. _____ yearly professional cleaning of file

34. _____ revolutions per minute

35. _____ used to make holes in the free edge of the nail

WORD REVIEW

If you do not know the meaning of the words listed below, look them up in the text.

bit	grit	torque
concentric	revolutions per minute (RPMs)	
flutes	rings of fire	

13

Aromatherapy

INTRODUCTION

1. List four reasons for adding aromatherapy to your salon.

   a. _____

   b. _____

   c. _____

   d. _____

2. Define aromatherapy.

   _____

   _____

3. List six ways aromatherapy can enhance your life.

   a. _____

   b. _____

   c. _____

   d. _____

   e. _____

   f. _____

4. Aromatherapy can be used for medicinal purposes, preventative health, _____ , and _____ .

ESSENTIAL OILS

5. a. Essential oils are extracted by various forms of _____ from botanical sources in various parts of the plant.

   b. List these botanical sources.

      1. _____

      2. _____

      3. _____

      4. _____

      5. _____

      6. _____

6. List five services in which essential oils can be incorporated.

    a. _____

    b. _____

    c. _____

    d. _____

    e. _____

7. Describe two improvements essential oils can have in manicures.

    a. _____

    b. _____

8. Essential oils can be used anywhere your _____.

TEN BASIC ESSENTIAL OILS

9. **Matching.** Match the essential oil on the left with its brief description on the right.

    _____ 1. Lavender   A. stimulating to circulation, astringent, overall first aid oil

    _____ 2. Chamomile   B. relieves pain, decongestant

    _____ 3. Marjoram   C. balancing to mind and body, tranquility

    _____ 4. Rosemary   D. antiviral, stimulant

    _____ 5. Tea Tree   E. digestive, soothes frayed nerves

    _____ 6. Cypress   F. antifungal, antibacterial

    _____ 7. Peppermint   G. antidepressant, water-retentive

    _____ 8. Eucalyptus   H. relaxant, balance

    _____ 9. Bergamot   I. comfort, menstrual cramps

    _____10. Geranium   J. clears sinuses, energy

10. Store essential oils in _____.

11. a. Keep essential oils away from _____.

    b. It can cause some oils to turn _____.

    c. They should never feel _____ or have a sick _____.

CARRIER OILS

12. Define carrier oil.

    _____

13. List two reasons why a carrier oil is helpful.

    a. _____

    b. _____

14. One oil that can be used directly on the skin is lavender as it can be used on _____.

15. Why should you do a patch test of an oil?

    _____

16. List five carrier oils

    a. _____

b. _____

c. _____

d. _____

e. _____

17. Which carrier oil has the longest shelf life?

_____

18. A client can help in the choice of the aroma used during a service if you gently pass the uncovered aroma under her _____ .

MATCHING REVIEW

Insert the correct word listed in front of each definition below.

allergic reaction   essential oils   light-sensitive glass
aromatherapy   geranium oil   patch test
carrier oils   jojoba oil   peppermint oil
chamomile oil   lavender   rancid
dedadent manicure   lemon oil   rose petals
diffusers   light rings   smells

19. _____ distilled from botanical sources

20. _____ oil that relaxes and is used as an overall first aid oil

21. _____ has the longest shelf life

22. _____ distinctive memories are associated with these

23. _____ added to make essential oils easier to use

24. _____ done to detect an allergic reaction

25. _____ need over a ton of these for one pound of oil

26. _____ essential oils are used in these

WORD REVIEW

If you do not know the meaning of the words listed below, look them up in the text.

aromatherapy   botanical
carrier oil   essential oil

Part 4

THE ART OF NAIL TECHNOLOGY

Nail Tips

INTRODUCTION

1. List three types of material out of which nail tips are made.

   a. _____

   b. _____

   c. _____

2. Name two other nail services with which nail tips are often combined.

   a. _____

   b. _____

3. A nail tip with no overlay is very _____. Consequently, it will not last long and is considered to be a/an _____ nail.

MATERIALS

4. What is a nail abrasive?

   _____

   _____

5. Define buffer block.

   _____

6. a. List two other names for nail adhesive.

   1. _____

   2. _____

   b. What is the purpose of this adhesive?

   _____

   c. Nail adhesive usually comes in a/an _____ with a pointed applicator _____.

7. a. On a nail tip, its point of contact with the client's nail plate is called the tip's _____.

   b. List two types of nail tip wells.

   1. _____

   2. _____

8. How much of a client's natural nail plate should a nail tip cover?

   _____

9. Define position stop.

_____

_____

NAIL TIP APPLICATION PRESERVICE

10. Besides the standard manicuring table, list four materials needed to apply nail tips.

   a. _____

   b. _____

   c. _____

   d. _____

11. What should you check for before the service begins?

_____

12. Label the half well, full well, and position stop on both pictures.

   1. _____

   2. _____

   3. _____

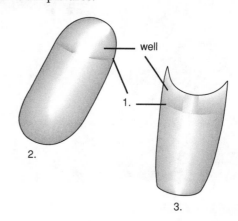

PROCEDURE

13. Under each of the following pictures, list the procedural step for applying nail tips that is shown.

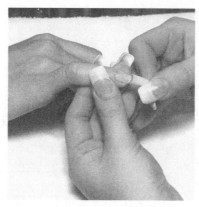
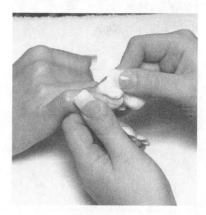

a. _____   b. _____   c. _____

_____   _____   _____

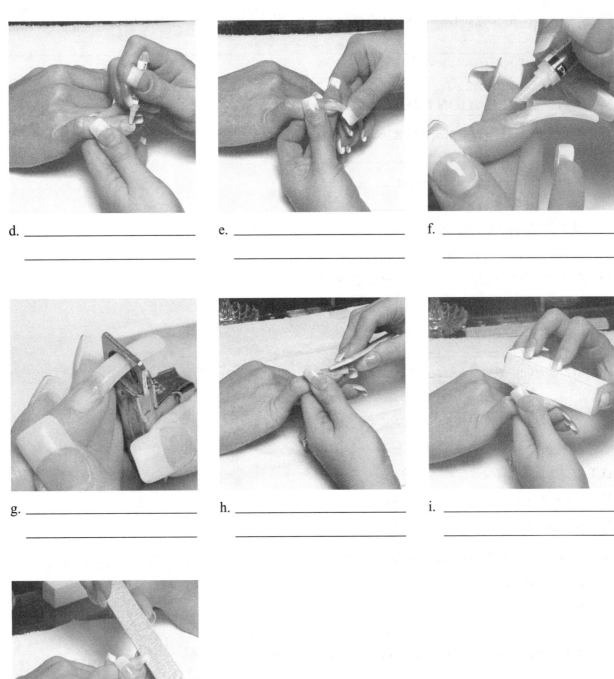

d. _____

_____

e. _____

_____

f. _____

_____

g. _____

_____

h. _____

_____

i. _____

_____

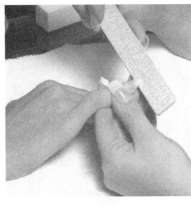

j. _____

_____

14. Besides sanitizing, list two other purposes of applying nail antiseptic.

a _____

b. _____

15. If you accidentally touch the nails after the antiseptic has been applied, you must _____ again.

16. Nail tips should cover the nail plate from sidewall to _____ .

17. Why is a bead of adhesive applied to the seam?

_____

18. a. Which implement is used to trim the nail to its desired length?

_____

   b. How should the nail tip be cut?

_____

   c. What happens if the tip is cut straight across with small nail clippers?

_____

19. a. When sanding the shine off of the nail tip, how should the file be held?

_____

   b. Why?

_____

20. Which implement is used to blend the tip into the nail plate?

_____

21. Which implement is used to shape the end of the new, longer nail?

_____

ALTERNATIVE TIP APPLICATION

22. Tip well cutting is an alternative method of achieving _____ .

23. For added strength, tips can be applied using _____ .

MAINTENANCE AND REMOVAL OF TIPS

24. List two reasons why clients with nail tips need regular maintenance.
   a. _____
   b. _____

25. If a client has nail tips, what type of nail polish remover is used?

_____

26. List two agents that will remove nail tips.
   a. _____
   b. _____

27. List the steps to remove nail tips.
   a. _____
   b. _____
   c. _____
   d. _____
   e. _____
   f. _____

MATCHING REVIEW

Insert the correct word/term listed in front of each definition below.

abrasive
acetone polish remover
antiseptic
buffer block

disinfectant
emery board
nail adhesive
nail tips

nonacetone polish remover
position stop
well

28. _____ a lightweight rectangular item that is abrasive and used to buff the nails

29. _____ made out of plastic, nylon, or acetate

30. _____ sanitizes, removes natural oil, and dehydrates the nail

31. _____ on a nail tip, the point of contact with the client's nail plate

32. _____ also called glue or bonding agent

33. _____ used to remove polish and not remove nail tips

34. _____ a rough surface used to shape or smooth the nail, and remove the shine

35. _____ point where the nail plate meets the tip before it is glued to the nail

WORD REVIEW

If you do not know the meaning of the words listed below, look them up in the text.

abrasive
acetate
acetone polish remover
bonding agent
buffer block
full well
glue

glue remover
nail adhesive
nail antiseptic
nail tip(s)
nonacetone polish remover
nylon
partial/half-well

plastic
position stop
seam
sidewall
stress point
well

15

Date _____

Rating _____

Text Pages 267–281

Nail Wraps

INTRODUCTION

1. Define nail wraps.

   _____

   _____

2. List two purposes of nail wraps.

   a. _____

   b. _____

3. Precut overlays have a/an _____.

4. a. List three types of fabric wraps.

   1. _____

   2. _____

   3. _____

   b. Which of the three fabric wraps is opaque, thereby needing colored polish to cover it after it is applied?

   _____

   c. Which of the three fabric wraps is transparent and may or may not need colored polish?

   _____

   d. Which of the three fabric wraps has a loose weave that makes it easy for the adhesive to protect?

   _____

5. a. List two chemicals that dissolve paper wraps.

   1. _____

   2. _____

   b. How often do paper wraps have to be replaced?

   _____

PROCEDURE FOR APPLYING FABRIC WRAPS

6. Besides your basic manicure table setup, list seven other materials you will need for applying fabric wraps.

   a. _____

   b. _____

   c. _____

d. _____

e. _____

f. _____

g. _____

7. Write in the steps of a nail wrap procedure. Some of them are completed for you.

a. __Remove old polish._____

b. _____

c. _____

d. _____

e. _____

f. _____

g. _____

h. __Cut fabric._____

i. _____

j. _____

k. _____

l. _____

m. _____

n. __Apply second coat of adhesive._____

o. _____

p. _____

q. _____

r. _____

s. __Apply polish._____

8. How far from the sidewalls and free edge should the fabric be trimmed?

_____

9. What sensation will the client feel if you get some adhesive dryer on the skin during the application?

_____

10. How do you apply the second coat of adhesive in order to prevent lifting?

_____

_____

_____

11. a. What two items do you use to buff the nails after the wraps are on?

1. _____

2. _____

b. Why do you buff the wrap(s)?

_____

   c. What can happen if you buff too much or too hard?

_____

12. How do you remove traces of oil from the nail?

_____

NAIL WRAP POST-SERVICE PROCEDURE

13. How do you clean clogged extender tips?

_____

_____

14. In most states, implements need to be sanitized for _____ minutes before they can be used on the next client.

FABRIC WRAP MAINTENANCE

15. a. Do you apply additional fabric to your client's wrap(s) two weeks after the wrap(s) were applied?

     _____

    b. In a two-week fabric wrap maintenance application, what do you apply to the new growth first, and then to the entire nail?

     _____

16. a. Do you apply additional fabric to your client's wrap(s) four weeks after the wrap(s) were applied?

     _____

    b. How is the procedure in question 16a above applied?

     _____

     _____

FABRIC WRAP REPAIR

17. List two reasons for fabric wrap repair.

    a. _____

    b. _____

18. Define repair patch.

_____

_____

19. How do you apply a repair patch?

_____

_____

FABRIC WRAP REMOVAL

20. Using the letters **A**, **B**, **C**, **D**, and **E**, put the following steps in correct sequential order to remove fabric wraps.

    _____ buff nails

    _____ soak nails

    _____ condition cuticles

    _____ complete nail wrap pre-service preparation

    _____ slide off softened wraps

21. To remove nail wraps, what do you soak the nails in?

    _____

22. a. When buffing the nails, what side of the block buffer is used?

    _____

    b. What does buffing remove?

    _____

PAPER WRAPS

23. What is the name of the thin paper used for paper wraps?

    _____

24. How long do paper wraps last?

    _____

25. Concerning paper wraps, what specifically does nail polish remover dissolve?

    _____

26. Why aren't paper wraps recommended for extra long nails?

    _____

MATERIALS

27. List three materials needed for paper wraps.

    a. _____

    b. _____

    c. _____

28. Mending liquid is applied with a/an _____ .

PAPER WRAP APPLICATION PROCEDURE

29. Below each diagram, list the correct procedural step for a paper wrap.

a. _____

_____

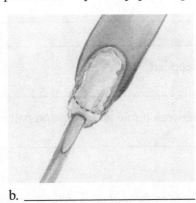

b. _____

_____

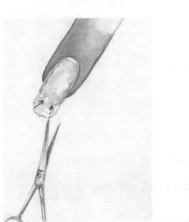

c. _____

_____

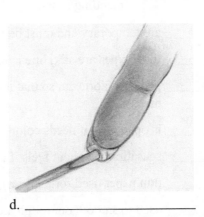

d. _____

_____

30. Is the mending liquid applied to the tissue before or after the tissue is applied to the client's nail(s)?

_____

31. Which implement is used to distribute the paper wrap smoothly on the nail?

_____

32. a. How many coats of mending liquid should be applied?

_____

b. List two places where the liquid should be applied.

1. _____

2. _____

33. a. To smooth the nail surface, apply a thin coat of

_____.

b. Before applying polish, this thin coat must be completely

_____.

LIQUID NAIL WRAP

34. Define liquid nail wrap.

_____

_____

35. How is liquid nail wrap applied?

_____

36. Explain the difference between liquid nail wrap and nail hardener.

_____

MATCHING REVIEW

Insert the correct word/term listed in front of each definition below.

acetone   fiberglass   nail adhesive
block buffer   heat   nail wraps
cold   linen   paper wraps
fabric wraps   mending tissue   repair patch

37. _____ are temporary and must be replaced when polish is removed.

38. _____ three types are silk, linen, and fiberglass

39. _____ piece of fabric cut so that it completely covers the crack or break in the nail

40. _____ is opaque so it needs colored polish when it is on the nails

41. _____ sensation the client feels if adhesive dryer gets on their skin

42. _____ thin paper used for paper wraps

43. _____ used to smooth out rough areas in the fabric

44. _____ has a loose weave so that adhesive penetrates easily

45. _____ used to remove nail wraps

46. _____ nail-size pieces of cloth or paper that are bonded to the front of the nail plate with nail adhesive

WORD REVIEW

If you do not know the meanings of the words listed below, look them up in the text.

abrasive   mending tissue   repair patch
adhesive dryer   nail adhesive/glue   ridge filler
adhesive extender tip   nail antiseptic   silk
fabric   nail block buffer   small scissors
fiberglass   nail wraps   stress strip
linen   opaque   transparent
liquid nail wrap   overlays
mending liquid   paper wraps

16

Acrylic Nails

INTRODUCTION

1. Another name for sculptured nails is _____ nails.

2. a. List two products from which sculptured nails are made.

   1. _____

   2. _____

   b. These two products form a wet _____ that can easily be molded into a nail
   _____ .

3. a. List three ingredients of acrylic nails.

   1. _____

   2. _____

   3. _____

   b. Of the three ingredients in question 3 above:

   1. acrylic liquid is a type of _____ .

   2. a finished acrylic nail is a _____ .

   3. an ingredient that speeds up the hardening process is a _____ .

4. The process whereby heat transfers from one polymer bead to the other, and continues until the last polymer bead receives heat, is called _____ .

5. Name two items that combine to make up the powder into which you dip your brush.

   a. _____

   b. _____

6. a. List two methods of applying acrylic nails.

   1. _____

   2. _____

   b. Which of the two methods looks like a French manicure and needs no polish?

   _____

   c. Which of the two methods creates a chalky white nail that needs colored polish or a clear, shiny coating that allows the natural nail to show through?

   _____

MATERIALS

7. Besides basic manicuring tools or equipment, list 16 other items needed to apply sculptured nails.

a. _____

b. _____

c. _____

d. _____

e. _____

f. _____

g. _____

h. _____

i. _____

j. _____

k. _____

l. _____

m. _____

n. _____

o. _____

p. _____

8. a. Why is primer used?

_____

b. List two types of primer.

1. _____

2. _____

c. Which type of primer is noninvasive to the natural nail?

_____

d. Which type of primer can cause serious damage to the skin and eyes?

_____

e. List two safety items you should wear when applying primer.

1. _____

2. _____

9. a. The two types of nail forms are reusable and

_____.

b. Which type of nail form in question 9a has an adhesive backing to hold it in place?

_____

c. Name two kinds of material out of which reusable nail forms are made.

1. _____

2. _____

10. What is used to apply and shape soft balls of acrylic on the nail?

_____

PROCEDURE

11. Which is applied first, primer or nail antiseptic?

_____

12. When positioning the nail form, the client's free edge is to be _____ the form.

13. Place the number 1, 2, 3, 4, 5, or 6 beside each diagram to show correct procedural order.

a. ___ Always wear safety glasses when applying primer.

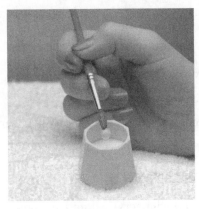

b. ___ Form ball of acrylic

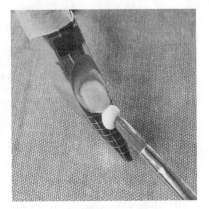

c. ___ Place ball of acrylic on nail form.

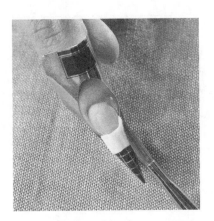

d. ___ Shape white into "smile."

e. ___ File sidewalls to free edge.

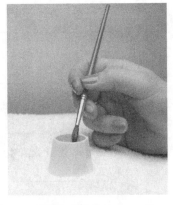

f. ___ Dip brush into acrylic liquid.

14. a. Where is the first ball of acrylic placed?

_____

b. Where is the second acrylic ball placed?

_____

15. What part of the sable brush is used to dab and press the acrylic?

_____

16. Define acrylic beads.

_____

_____

17. a. How do you know when the acrylic nail is dry?

_____

b. When the nails are dry, what is the next step?

_____

18. Assume that you have just removed the nail forms. Use the letters **A**, **B**, **C**, **D**, **E**, **F**, and **G** to show the correct order of the following steps.

_____ clean nails

_____ buff the acrylic nail with block buffer

_____ apply polish

_____ clean up your work area or table

_____ apply oil to cuticles

_____ shape the free edge of the acrylic nail with a coarse or medium abrasive

_____ apply cream and perform massage

ACRYLIC APPLICATION POSTSERVICE PROCEDURE

19. After the service, what do you do with acrylic liquid and powder left in the small containers?

_____

20. Name two items that can be used to clean your sable brush.

a. _____

b. _____

21. Bristles should not be pulled out of a brush because

_____

22. a. How should acrylic powders be stored?

_____

b. What two items are to be stored in cool, dark places?

1. _____

2. _____

c. Acrylic nail products should not be stored near

_____.

ACRYLIC APPLICATION OVER TIPS OR NATURAL NAILS

23. **Matching.** The left column contains the correct acrylic nail procedure. Match these items with their specific descriptions, directions, or characteristics listed in the right column. The first one is done for you.

___*(E)*___ 1. push cuticle back   A. wear plastic gloves and safety glasses

_____ 2. buff to remove shine   B. dip briefly in liquid soap and water

_____ 3. clean nails   C. place on nail plate

_____ 4. apply nail antiseptic   D. rub into cuticles and surrounding skin

_____ 5. apply tips   E. use a light touch because the cuticle is dry

_____ 6. apply primer

_____ 7. prepare liquid and powder

_____ 8. dip brush into liquid and powder

_____ 9. place first ball

_____ 10. place second ball

_____ 11. apply acrylic beads

_____ 12. shape nail

_____ 13. buff nail

_____ 14. apply cuticle oil

_____ 15. massage hands and arms

_____ 16. apply polish

F. pick up medium, dry ball

G. base coat, polish, top coat

H. attach plastic nails to client's natural nails

I. small wet balls used to smooth entire acrylic surface.

J. use medium/fine file to remove natural oil(s)

K. use block buffer to smooth entire acrylic surface

L. use in small, separate containers

M. place on nail's free edge

N. use orangewood stick, cotton, or spray to prevent bacteria growth

O. use coarse abrasive on the free edge

P. use hand cream or lotion

ACRYLIC BACKFILL

24. The term backfill applies to the _____ of the white free edge.

25. The basic backfill procedure should be performed _____.

26. List the two different ways to replace a new smile line.

    a. _____

    b. _____

27. Explain the four-step procedure using an electric file.

    a. _____

    b. _____

    c. _____

    d. _____

28. Explain the two-step procedure without using an electric file.

    a. _____

    _____

    b. _____

    _____

ACRYLIC NAIL APPLICATION OVER BITTEN NAILS

29. Explain the difference in applying acrylics over bitten nails compared with applying acrylics over forms.

    _____

    _____

30. Where is the first ball of acrylic applied?

    _____

31. What is done after this first ball of acrylic has been shaped and dried?

    _____

32. Explain where a nail form is placed.

    _____

33. Once the nail forms are on, the procedure follows the same steps as for acrylic nails over

    _____ .

ACRYLIC NAIL MAINTENANCE

34. List two things that regular maintenance of acrylic nails helps to prevent.

    a. _____

    b. _____

35. Explain what can happen if a client does not maintain acrylic nails.

    _____

    _____

36. Define rebalancing.

    _____

37. Define acrylic fills.

    _____

38. How often should acrylic nails be filled?

    _____

39 List the missing steps in the following procedure for acrylic nail fills.

    a. _Remove old polish._____

    b. _____

    c. _Refine, then buff the nail._____

    d. _____

    e. _Clean the nail._____

    f. _____

    g. _Remove the shine from the natural nail surface._____

    h. _____

    i. _Apply primer._____

    j. _____

    k. _Place and shape balls of acrylic._____

    l. _Shape, then buff the nail._____

    m._____

    n. _Apply hand cream, and massage hand and arm._____

    o. _____

    p. _Apply polish._____

40. a. Should a nipper be used to cut away loose acrylic?

_____

   b. Why or why not?

_____

41. Explain what should be done if a client has excessive or a lot of acrylic lifting.

_____

_____

ACRYLIC CRACK REPAIR

42. Define acrylic crack repair.

_____

_____

43. List two ways the cracked acrylic can be filed.

   a. _____

   b. _____

44. In performing an acrylic crack repair, when would a nail form be used?

_____

45. Where are the first balls or beads of acrylic placed or applied?

_____

ACRYLIC REMOVAL

46. List five steps to removing acrylics.

   a. _____

   b. _____

   c. _____

   d. _____

   e. _____

47. The client's fingertips should be soaked for _____ minutes or as long as needed to _____ the acrylic product. For acrylic removal, refer to the _____ directions.

ODORLESS ACRYLICS

48. a. Shaping odorless acrylics can be done at a _____ pace than traditional acrylics.

   b. Drying time is _____.

49. Explain the self-leveling characteristics of odorless acrylics.

_____

50. a. What is the surface like when odorless acrylics are dry?

_____

   b. What happens to this residue as you refine the nails?

_____

51. Explain why traditional and odorless acrylic products cannot be mixed together.

_____

LIGHT-CURED ACRYLICS

52. Light-cured acrylics are similar to odorless acrylics with _____ as an added feature.

53. a. These trigger the chemicals to harden when exposed to a _____.

    b. They don't evaporate so they also are _____.

    c. They _____ be mixed with other products.

COLORED ACRYLICS

54. Acrylics are manufactured "clear," and then _____ are added.

55. a. The more white added, the more _____ the color becomes.

    b. The less white added, the _____ the color remains.

56. Nail artistry on the acrylic nail is limited only by your _____.

DIPPING METHOD

57. List the three products used during the dipping method

    a. _____

    b. _____

    c. _____

MATCHING REVIEW

Insert the correct word listed in front of each definition below.

acrylic	monomer	polymerization
catalyst	nonetching	primer
curing	pigment	rebalancing
disposable forms	photoinitiators	reusable forms
etching	polymer	sable brush

58. _____ ingredient that speeds up the hardening process

59. _____ type of primer that can damage the skin and eyes

60. _____ process of forming the nail

61. _____ another name for sculptured nails

62. _____ redefining the contour of the nail

63. _____ made out of aluminum, Teflon, or plastic

64. _____ example is acrylic liquid

65. _____ type of primer that can be used safely

66. _____ added to clear acrylic to color it

67. _____ used to apply and shape soft balls of acrylic on the nail

68. _____ trigger chemicals to harden under a U. V. light

WORD REVIEW

If you do not know the meanings of the words listed below, look them up in the text.

acetone

acrylic beads

acrylic liquid

acrylic maintenance

acrylic nails

acrylic powder

ball of acrylic

bitten nails

catalyst

crack repair

curing

dipping method

etching

light-cured acrylics

liquid soap

monomer

nail antiseptic

nail forms

nonacetone

nonetching

odorless acrylics

one-color method

pigment

polymer

polymerization

primer

rebalancing

sable brush

safety glasses

sculptured nails

self-leveling

two-color method

17

Gels

INTRODUCTION

1. List two types of gel nails.

   a. _____

   b. _____

2. Which type of gel is hardened by a special light source?

   _____

3. The source of this special light is _____.

4. Explain how no-light gels harden.

   _____

5. **True/False.** The following statements concern the color of gel nails. Mark the true statements with a **T** and the false statements with an **F**.

   _____ 1. Gels are available in colors that do not need polish.

   _____ 2. Colored gels are not a base for nail art.

   _____ 3. Polish will permanently change the color of gel.

   _____ 4. Gel nails must always be polished.

   _____ 5. Polish may be worn over colored gels.

   _____ 6. Colored gels are a great base for nail art.

   _____ 7. Gels stay the same color until the gel is removed.

   _____ 8. Polish cannot be worn over gels.

MATERIALS NEEDED FOR LIGHT-CURED GEL APPLICATION

6. List eight items needed for gel nails.

   a. _____   e. _____

   b. _____   f. _____

   c. _____   g. _____

   d. _____   h. _____

7. What is a curing light?

   _____

   _____

GEL APPLICATION PRE-SERVICE PROCEDURE

8. Before applying gels, the client's nails are to be dehydrated with a/an _____.

LIGHT-CURED GEL PROCEDURE

9. **Directions.** Using the list on top, fill in the bottom list with the application for light-cured gels in their correct procedural steps.

Apply top coat of gel	Apply cream and perform	Cure third coat of gel
Clean nails	massage	Apply cuticle oil
Push back cuticles	Remove polish	Apply polish
Apply building gel	Clean nails	Cure second coat of gel
Apply tips	Apply nail prep	Apply nail antiseptic
Cure base coat of gel	Buff nails to remove shine	Clean nails
Apply small amount of gel	Final nail buffing	Apply base coat of gel
again	Buff nails to remove residue	Check nail contours

a. _____

b. _____

c. _____

d. _____

e. _____

f. _____

g. _____

h. _____

i. _____

j. _____

k. _____

l. _____

m. _____

n. _____

o. _____

p. _____

q. _____

r. _____

s. _____

t. _____

u. _____

v. _____

10. Gel is applied to the nail by brushing it on in a thin, _____ layer.

11. The gel will lift if it is brushed onto the _____.

12. How do you know the amount of minutes needed under the gel light?

_____

13. An inadequately sheilded ultraviolet lamp can cause damage to the _____ and skin.

GEL APPLICATION POST-SERVICE PROCEDURE

14. List five things you are to do after completing a gel nail application.

    a. _____

    b. _____

    c. _____

    d. _____

    e. _____

15. In most states, sanitizing implements means that before using them on the next client, items are to be sanitized for _____ minutes.

LIGHT-CURED GEL APPLIED ON FORMS

16. Fill in the missing procedural steps for light-cured gels applied onto nail forms.

    a. __Apply nail forms._____

    b. _____

    c. __Cure the gel._____

    d. _____

    e. __Cure the gel._____

    f. _____

    g. __Cure the gel._____

    h. __Remove the forms._____

    i. _____

    j. __Apply gel to the entire nail without the form._____

    k. _____

    l. __Remove tacky residue._____

    m. _____

    n. _____

    o. _____

    p. _____

    q. _____

    r. _____

    s. _____

    t. __Apply hand cream and perform massage._____

    u. _____

    v. __Apply polish._____

17. What is meant by "remove residue?"

    _____

    _____

18. Below each figure, list the procedural step that is shown.

 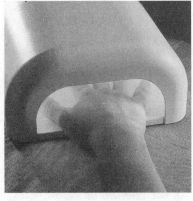 

a. _____
   _____

b. _____
   _____

c. _____
   _____

PROCEDURE FOR NO-LIGHT GEL APPLICATION

19. List two no-light curing agents.

    a. _____

    b. _____

20. Because curing agents vary for no-light gels, it is essential that you read and follow the _____ directions.

21. a. If the gels are water-cured, the temperature of the water should be _____ .

    b. Depending on the manufacturers' directions, water-cured gels should be immersed for _____ to _____ minutes.

22. a. What is another name for spray or brush gel activator?

    _____

    b. A spray gel activator should be held _____ inches away from the client's _____ . This is to reduce the chance of the client experiencing a _____ reaction from the activator.

23. No-light gels can be combined with a _____ wrap for added strength.

24. The wrap is added between the _____ and _____ coats of gel.

25. The wrap pieces cut will form a/an _____ .

GEL MAINTENANCE

26. How often should gel nails be maintained?

    _____

27. Before applying new gel, the old gel must be buffed. You buff until

    _____ .

28. a. Explain how the file should be held for buffing.

    _____

    b. Why should you hold the file in this way?

    _____

29. After the buffing is completed, what procedure is followed to maintain the gels?

_____

GEL REMOVAL

30. How would you remove a light-cured gel?

_____

31. If the client has no-light gels, the nails should be _____ in acetone. Then the softened gel should be gently pushed off using a/an _____.

MATCHING REVIEW

Insert the correct word listed in front of each definition below.

acetone	light-cured	ultraviolet
adhesive dryer	liquid	safety glasses
apron	lukewarm	steel pusher
cold	orangewood stick	
curing light	regrowth ledge	

32. _____ nails hardened by a special light source

33. _____ a product that will remove no-light gel nails

34. _____ box with ultraviolet bulbs to cure or harden gel nails

35. _____ another name for spray or brush gel activator

36. _____ type of soap used to wash client's hands

37. _____ type of light that can harm the eyes and skin

38. _____ temperature of water to cure gels

39. _____ area to be removed in gel maintenance

40. _____ used to gently slide off softened gel tip

WORD REVIEW

If you do not know the meanings of the words listed below, look them up in the text.

adhesive dryer	gels	regrowth ledge
brush gel activator	halogen light	spray gel activator
cure	light-cured gels	ultraviolet light
curing light	no-light gels	

18

The Creative Touch

THE BASICS

1. List the four basic rules that will lead to success in your creative endeavor.

   a. _____

   b. _____

   c. _____

   d. _____

2. Schedule ample _____ for art services. Display nail art designs suited to the _____ and the _____. Be competitively _____ and invest in _____ tools.

3. List the four classifications of color that will aid you in selecting polish and paint colors.

   a. _____

   b. _____

   c. _____

   d. _____

CREATING NAIL ART

4. List five types/tools of nail art.

   a. _____

   b. _____

   c. _____

   d. _____

   e. _____

5. To interest clients in nail art, you might want to wear artistic designs on _____ nails.

6. **Identification.** Using the letters **GL**, **G**, **T**, **F**, **A**, and **H** (defined below), match the correct characteristics listed below with one form of nail art.
   Key:
   GL = gold leafing
   G = gems
   T = striping tape
   F = foil
   A = airbrushing
   H = handpainted (flat nail art)

Characteristics:

_____ 1. comes in fragile sheets

_____ 2. comes in rolls and is applied to an adhesive

_____ 3. uses stencils

_____ 4. gives sparkle and texture, and is applied to tacky top coat

_____ 5. uses brushstrokes to achieve a design

_____ 6. comes in very thin rolls with an adhesive backing

_____ 7. can be reused if the silver backing is in place

_____ 8. also known as nuggets

_____ 9. shiny colored side faces up

_____10. paint is sprayed through a gun using a compressor

_____11. applied to a dry, polished nail

_____12. two colors can be used at the same time on one brush

FREEHAND PAINTING

7.   Freehand painting is also known as _____.

8.   List seven types of brushes used in freehand painting.

   a. _____

   b. _____

   c. _____

   d. _____

   e. _____

   f. _____

   g. _____

9.   Another name for a marbilizer is a _____.

10. Brush strokes are accomplished by mastering what three basics?

   a. _____

   b. _____

   c. _____

11. The technique of airbrushing two or more colors on the nail at the same time is called the
   _____ or _____.

12. How does an airbrush work?

   _____

13. List three ways in which airbrushes differ.

   a. _____

   b. _____

   c. _____

14. When learning airbrush techniques, practice them on what three surfaces?

    a. _____

    b. _____

    c. _____

15. Write in the steps of an airbrushing procedure. Some of them are completed for you.

    a. ___Complete the nail service and have client pay bill prior to airbrush service.___

    b. _____

    c. _____

    d. ___Airbrush nails.___

    e. _____

    f. _____

    g. _____

    h. ___Cleanse the fingers or toes.___

    i. _____

16. List two popular airbrush techniques.

    a. _____

    b. _____

MATCHING REVIEW

Insert the correct word listed in front of each definition below.

absorbent paper	flat nail art	nail art
acetone	foil	sealer
airbrush	gems	steel pusher
color fade	gold leafing	striping tape
design tool	mask knife	tweezers

17. _____ made of very fragile sheets

18. _____ includes gems, foil, striping tape, airbrushing, and flat nail art

19. _____ a compressor that pushes air through a gun

20. _____ used to place gems on nails

21. _____ comes in very thin rolls with an adhesive backing

22. _____ popular airbrush technique

23. _____ good for practicing airbrushing

24. _____ applied over most nail art

25. _____ brushes and strokework help create this type of art

26. _____ a marbelizer or stylus

27. _____ used to create nail art stencils

28. _____ best for removing airbrushed nail color

WORD REVIEW

If you do not know the meanings of the words listed below, look them up in the text.

air hose	freehand painting	nail art
air source	French manicure	nail glaze
airbrush	gems	overspray
color blend	gold leafing	paint bonder
color fade	gravity-fed	pearlescent paint
compressor	internal mix	reservoir
design tool	mask knife	striping tape
foil	mask paper	stencil

THE BUSINESS OF NAIL TECHNOLOGY

19

Date _____

Rating _____

Text Pages 357–371

Salon Business

INTRODUCTION

1. To be financially successful, a nail technician must not only know how to perform nail services well, but must also be a well-rounded _____ person.

2. List six expenses a salon owner incurs.

   a. _____

   b. _____

   c. _____

   d. _____

   e. _____

   f. _____

YOUR WORKING ENVIRONMENT

3. **Identification.** Using the letters **FS**, **NO**, **TS**, and **DS** (defined below), match the correct characteristics listed below with one type of salon.
   Key:
   FS = full-service salon
   NO = nails-only salon
   TS = tanning salon
   DS = day spa
   Characteristics:

   _____ 1. rapid client growth

   _____ 2. often employ only one nail technician

   _____ 3. you automatically get all of the nail care business

   _____ 4. you will work with other nail technicians

   _____ 5. clients who like tranquil surroundings

   _____ 6. clients coming in every 15 minutes

   _____ 7. more likely to use low-order products

   _____ 8. clients may take nail care more seriously

4. Briefly list eleven items you should consider when deciding on a salon that is right for you.

   a. _____

   b. _____

   c. _____

d. _____

e. _____

f. _____

g. _____

h. _____

i. _____

j. _____

k. _____

_____

KEEPING GOOD PERSONAL RECORDS

5. List four business/financial items you should save.

   a. _____

   b. _____

   c. _____

   d. _____

6. a. Define income.

   _____

   b. List four sources of salon income.

   1. _____

   2. _____

   3. _____

   4. _____

7. a. Define expenses.

   _____

   b. List six salon expenses.

   1. _____

   2. _____

   3. _____

   4. _____

   5. _____

   6. _____

BOOTH RENTER/SALON OWNERSHIP

8. Someone who rents space in a salon is considered to be an independent contractor or a

   _____ .

9. Some states have _____ this practice.

10. List three duties a booth renter performs.

    a. _____

    b. _____

    c. _____

11. List two ways to become a salon owner.

    a. _____

    b. _____

INTERVIEW

12. Define interview.

    _____

13. List eight ways that contribute to making a good first impression.

    a. _____

    b. _____

    c. _____

    d. _____

    e. _____

    f. _____

    g. _____

    h. _____

14. Define resume.

    _____

15. List the five main parts of a resume.

    a. _____

    b. _____

    c. _____

    d. _____

    e. _____

UNDERSTANDING SALON BUSINESS RECORDS

16. Explain four reasons for keeping accurate business records.

    a. _____

    b. _____

    c. _____

    d. _____

    _____

17. **Identification.** Using the numbers **1** and **7** (defined below), match the correct type of business record with the number of years it should be kept.
    Key:
    1 = business records should be kept for at least 1 year
    7 = business records should be kept for at least 7 years

    _____ 1. monthly and yearly records

    _____ 2. daily sales slips

    _____ 3. cancelled checks

    _____ 4. inventory records

    _____ 5. appointment book

    _____ 6. payroll book

    _____ 7. petty cash book

    _____ 8. service records

18. **Matching.** Match the terms on the left with their correct descriptions on the right.

    _____ 1. inventory

    _____ 2. retail supplies

    _____ 3. changes in demands for services

    _____ 4. personal appointment records

    _____ 5. consumption supplies

    _____ 6. profit and loss comparisons

    _____ 7. service record

    _____ 8. net income

    A. over a period of time to see the slow versus busiest months

    B. supplies sold

    C. tells you who your next client is and what service you are to perform

    D. your income minus expenses

    E. the money you make

    F. if not successful, you may decide to cut that service from your business

    G. being a salaried employee versus an independent contractor

    H. with accurate records, you can cut costs by keeping appropriate stock levels and detect loss from theft

    I. supplies used in the business

    J. the money you spend

    K. a list of treatments given and merchandise sold to each client

BOOKING APPOINTMENTS

19. List six items that are needed to supply the appointment desk/book.

    a. _____

    b. _____

    c. _____

    d. _____

    e. _____

    f. _____

20. a. When acknowledging your client's presence at the counter, try not to keep them _____.

b. When answering the phone, identify both yourself and the salon by _____.

c. Let clients know you are _____ to talk with them.

d. Don't mumble or shout, but speak _____ to the client.

e. If you have appointments made in advance, it is a good practice to _____ your clients the night before the appointment to _____ them and confirm the _____ .

f. At the end of their appointment, always ask your clients if they wish to _____ .

21. What five items are to be written in the appointment book when a client makes an appointment?

a. _____

b. _____

c. _____

d. _____

e. _____

ADVERTISING YOURSELF

22. a. List three items that are to be included on a list of every service you offer.

1. _____

2. _____

3. _____

b. In what two places should you distribute this service list?

1. _____

2. _____

COLLECTING PAYMENT FOR SERVICES

23. In some salons, payments for services are collected by the _____ , while in other salons it is collected by the _____ .

24. List four items to be included on a client ticket.

a. _____

b. _____

c. _____

d. _____

WHERE TO GO

25. List six sources you might use in your endeavor to become the very best nail technician possible.

a. _____

b. _____

c. _____

d. _____

e. _____

f. _____

MATCHING REVIEW

Insert the correct word listed in front of each definition below.

appointment book	expenses	net worth
business	full-service	retail
client ticket	income	service list
consumption	inventory	service record
day spa	nails-only	

26. _____ should include a description of the service, length of time the service takes, and cost of the service

27. _____ supplies used in the business

28. _____ your assets minus your liabilities

29. _____ where the nail technician automatically gets all of the nail care business

30. _____ what you spend

31. _____ list of treatments given and merchandise sold to each client

32. _____ should include client's name, date, service performed, and cost

33. _____ where clients may take nail care more seriously

34. _____ the money you make

35. _____ supplies sold

36. _____ clients come in every 15 minutes

WORD REVIEW

If you do not know the meanings of the words listed below, look them up in the text.

accountant	income	receipts
advertising	income tax	receptionist
appointment book	independent contractor	rent
benefits	insurance	reputation
booth	inventory	retail supplies
buy	invoices	salary
cancelled checks	laws (local, state, and federal)	service record
check stubs	liability	sick days
commission	life insurance	social security
consumption supplies	loss	taxes
daily sales slips	nails-only salon	tips
disability insurance	net worth	tuition
dress code	payroll book	unemployment insurance
employee	personal appointment record	uniform
expenses	petty cash book	ventilation
full-service salon	profit	

20

Date _____

Rating _____

Text Pages 373–386

Selling Nail Products and Services

INTRODUCTION

1. List two things nail technicians are responsible for selling.

    a. _____

    b. _____

2. To be successful, the one basic selling goal is

    _____

3. List five basic steps to selling.

    a. _____

    b. _____

    c. _____

    d. _____

    e. _____

KNOW YOUR PRODUCTS AND SERVICES

4. a. Define feature.

    _____

   b. You learn product features by _____ labels, product bulletins, and industry literature.

   c. What information do you look for on these labels, bulletins, and literature?

       1. _____

       2. _____

       3. _____

       4. _____

5. List five features of nail services.

    a. _____

    b. _____

    c. _____

    d. _____

    e. _____

6. Define benefits.

   _____

7. You will be a good salesperson when you turn the _____ of your products and services into _____ that meet the client's needs and desires.

KNOW WHAT YOUR CLIENT NEEDS AND WANTS

8. When are your client's nail needs discovered or learned?

   _____

9. List four questions you will need your client to answer.

   a. _____

   b. _____

   c. _____

   d. _____

10. What are two important client lifestyle considerations?

    a. _____

    b. _____

MARKETING

11. List the three things involved in marketing a product or service.

    a. _____

    b. _____

    c. _____

12. Successful technicians never stop marketing _____.

13. List five methods of salon marketing.

    a. _____

    b. _____

    c. _____

    d. _____

    e. _____

14. Pricing professional products sold in the salon should be _____ the wholesale price.

15. Salons build employee raises into their pricing structure by having a _____.

16. A new technician would charge a _____ price.

17. Give two examples of salon literature.

    a. _____

    b. _____

18. Advertising your talents or those of your salon can be accomplished in at least five different ways. List them.

    a. _____

    b. _____

    c. _____

d. _____

e. _____

19. Ongoing promotions can be tied into _____ throughout the year.

PRESENTING YOUR PRODUCTS AND SERVICES

20. What are two opportunities to sell products and services?

    a. _____

    b. _____

21. While performing a service, tell the client what _____ you are using and why. Suggest that she _____ certain product types and tell her how to use the products. Also discuss other services and the features, _____ , and costs of each.

22. List five items that can be included on a service list.

    a. _____

    b. _____

    c. _____

    d. _____

    e. _____

23. While having a service performed, an attractive product display should be in _____ of the client.

24. List five nail maintenance retail products.

    a. _____

    b. _____

    c. _____

    d. _____

    e. _____

ANSWER QUESTIONS AND OBJECTIONS

25. In order to answer client questions, you must be as _____ as possible about your products and services.

26. a. Discuss four items to which a client might object.

    1. _____

    2. _____

    3. _____

    4. _____

    b. You should answer the objection honestly and _____ , describing the advantages of the product or service, and weighing them against the _____ .

CLOSE THE SALE

27. List three steps to closing a sale.

    a. _____

    b. _____

    c. _____

28. What two items should be included on a business card given to the client for the next appointment?

    a. _____

    b. _____

TRACKING YOUR SUCCESS

29. Successful nail technicians have _____ and a _____ clientele.

30. a. A client who comes in at the same time and day for each appointment is said to have a
    _____ .

    b. They are less likely to _____ their appointment when it is the same day and time every week.

COMPLETION REVIEW

Insert the correct word listed in the sentences below.

appointment	level system	selling
benefit	needs	standing
client consultation	opening a sale	view
closing a sale	products	wearability
feature	reading	

31. For success, the one basic selling goal is to meet the _____ of your clients.

32. You learn from product labels, bulletins, and industry literature by _____ them.

33. What a product will do for your client, or how it will fulfill your client's needs and wants, is a/an
    _____ .

34. An appointment the same day and time each week is called a _____ .

35. Suggestive selling, wrap-up, and scheduling another _____ are three steps to
    _____ .

36. A specific fact about a product or service that describes it is a/an _____ .

37. While having a service performed, an attractive product display should be within the client's
    _____ .

38. Your client's nail needs and wants are discovered or learned during the _____ .

39. Employee raises can be accomplished by using a _____ in the salon.

WORD REVIEW

If you do not know the meanings of the words listed below, look them up in the text.

advantages

benefits

business card

client consultation

close the sale

disadvantages

display

features

industry literature

ingredients

labels

lifestyle

maintenance

nail look

nail problems

presenting products and services

product bulletins

products

objections

questions

safety precautions

salesperson

schedule another appointment

sell

service

services

suggested selling

wearability

wrap-up

Final Review

MULTIPLE CHOICE EXAMINATION

Directions: Read each statement carefully. Choose the best response from the four choices, A, B, C, or D.

1. The thin line of skin at the base of the nail that extends from the nail wall to the nail plate is the

   A. eponychium.

   B. hyponychium.

   C. free edge.

   D. nail groove. _____

2. The type of bacteria that does not produce disease and is often beneficial is

   A. spirilla.

   B. bacilla.

   C. pathogenic.

   D. nonpathogenic. _____

3. John is receiving a pedicure. His toenails should be shaped

   A. straight across with the corners rounded.

   B. into a curved shape.

   C. center to corner.

   D. into a pointed shape. _____

4. On a nail tip, the point where the nail plate meets the tip before it is glued to the nail is called the

   A. buffer block.

   B. position stop.

   C. half-well.

   D. full well. _____

5. Another name for a kneading massage movement is

   A. effleurage.

   B. friction.

   C. tapotement.

   D. petrissage. _____

6. Marion has nail wraps on her nails that are opaque and needs colored polish on them. This type of wrap is

    A. linen.

    B. fiberglass.

    C. silk.

    D. none of the above.   _____

7. Polish will not stain the nails if the nail technician applies

    A. a top coat.

    B. less than two coats of colored polish.

    C. nonacetone polish remover.

    D. a base coat.   _____

8. Tim is studying myology, which is the study of

    A. nerves.

    B. bones.

    C. skin.

    D. muscles.   _____

9. Catherine is performing a hand massage on her client Jacquie. The two layers of Jacquie's skin are

    A. papillary and dermis.

    B. papillary and stratum corneum.

    C. dermis and epidermis.

    D. epidermis and stratum corneum.   _____

10. The finished acrylic nail on Laura is a/an

    A. monomer.

    B. polymer.

    C. catalyst.

    D. adhesive.   _____

11. Mai uses odorless acrylic nails. A difference between odorless and traditional acrylics is that odorless nails

    A. dry faster than traditional acrylics.

    B. can be mixed with any traditional acrylic product.

    C. have no residue when they dry.

    D. are self-leveling.   _____

12. Debbie, a salon owner, is adding up the money she has spent on equipment, supplies, and uniforms. Debbie is totaling her

    A. profit and loss comparisons.

    B. income.

    C. expenses.

    D. net worth.   _____

13. During a pedicure procedure, the feet are soaked

    A. after the nails are shaped.

    B. at the beginning of the pedicure service.

    C. after the feet are massaged.

    D. immediately before the top coat is applied.   _____

14. An example of a vegetable parasite is

    A. pediculosis.

    B. ringworm.

    C. scabies.

    D. lice.   _____

15. Becca's Nail Salon has installed new ventilation. This ventilation is important for nail technicians and clients because nail products

    A. are flammable.

    B. only come in aerosol sprays.

    C. can cause viral infections.

    D. enter the body through inhalation.   _____

16. Monique's acrylic nails are curing. This means that they are

    A. softening.

    B. weakening.

    C. hardening.

    D. shrinking.   _____

17. The hair-like projections by which bacteria move are called

    A. mitosis.

    B. cocci.

    C. spores.

    D. flagella.   _____

Situation for Items 18 to 20:   *The following four clients have entered your nail salon. Kim, in for a manicure, has white spots on her nail plate. Dick's feet have ringworm, and he has blisters and inflammation, but would like a pedicure today. Mary has bitten, deformed nails and would like nail tips applied to her natural nails. Peter's nails curve over his nail tip/free edge, and he has an appointment for a manicure.*

18. Kim's condition is called

    A. onychauxis.

    B. leukonychia.

    C. onychorrhexis.

    D. agnails.   _____

19. Peter's nail condition is called

    A. nail mold.

    B. onychia.

    C. tinea pedis.

    D. onychogryposis.   _____

20. The nail technician should refuse to perform a nail service on

    A. Dick.

    B. Kim and Mary.

    C. Dick and Peter.

    D. Mary, Peter, and Kim.   _____

21. The nail service where acrylic is added to Karen's new growth area is called

    A. lifting.

    B. fill.

    C. crack repair.

    D. acrylic beads.   _____

22. Nails of adults grow at an average of

    A. 1/8 of an inch per week.

    B. 3mm per month.

    C. 1/20 of an inch per week.

    D. 1/16 of an inch per month.   _____

23. In the matrix are found blood vessels and

    A. lunula.

    B. nerves.

    C. hyponychiums.

    D. cartilage.   _____

24. An infected nail should be treated by a

    A. nail technician.

    B. physician.

    C. pharmacist.

    D. cosmetologist.   _____

25. In most states, instruments sanitized with hospital-grade disinfectant should be immersed for
    _____ minutes.

    A. 8

    B. 10

    C. 20

    D. 30   _____

26. The purpose of buffing the nail before applying an acrylic nail is to

    A. remove natural oil.

    B. add color to the nail.

    C. remove acrylic residue.

    D. add gloss to the nail.

27. Hangnails are treated by softening the cuticle with

    A. oil.

    B. polish remover.

    C. pumice.

    D. alum.

28. The digital bones of the fingers are called

    A. metatarsi.

    B. metacarpi.

    C. phalanges.

    D. clavicles.

29. The nevus on Vern's nail was probably caused by:

    A. high blood pressure.

    B. a pigmented mole that occurs in the nail.

    C. poor blood circulation.

    D. the natural immune system.

30. Brenda's local beauty supply distributor has given her a Material Data Safety Sheet for the product she uses. This sheet provides information on the product's

    A. instructions on how to apply.

    B. chemistry, hazards, and handling procedures.

    C. required sanitation policies and procedures.

    D. percentage of allergic reactions to it.

31. Charlotte has a light-cured gel system in her salon. Two light sources for these gels are

    A. ultraviolet and halogen.

    B. ultraviolet and infrared.

    C. infrared and halogen.

    D. visible and infrared.

32. The technical term for the nail is

    A. hyponychium.

    B. onyx.

    C. matrix.

    D. cura.

33. Ginny's nails will grow faster

    A. in the winter.

    B. as she gets older.

    C. in the summer.

    D. on her feet.

    _____

34. All of the following statements are true concerning AIDS *except* that it

    A. attacks the body's immune system.

    B. is caused by a virus.

    C. lies dormant for many years.

    D. is caused by bacteria.

    _____

35. Suk is explaining to Cheryl that a particular hand lotion will meet all of Cheryl's needs for her dry hands. Suk, the nail technician, is discussing the hand lotion's

    A. disadvantages.

    B. benefits.

    C. wrap-ups.

    D. features.

    _____

36. The part of Peggy's nail plate that extends over her fingertips is called the

    A. free edge.

    B. matrix.

    C. hyponychium.

    D. nail bed.

    _____

37. The ulna is the large bone on the little finger side of the

    A. wrist.

    B. hand.

    C. upper arm

    D. forearm.

    _____

38. Before using any manicuring implement, Randy should

    A. wipe it with tissue.

    B. wipe it with a towel.

    C. disinfect it.

    D. wash it with soap and hot water.

    _____

39. Melinda is performing a manicure using hot oil and an electric heater. The type of manicure Melinda is performing is

    A. plain water.

    B. French.

    C. reconditioning.

    D. electric.

    _____

40. Kay's nail problem is known as

   A. pseudomonas aeruginosa.

   B. carcinogenic.

   C. rickettsia.

   D. onychophagy.   _____

41. Given Kay's situation, the nail technician should

   A. work on Kay's nails after washing them with a liquid soap.

   B. first soak her nails in alcohol for 20 minutes.

   C. first soak her nails in acetone for 20 minutes.

   D. remove the artificial nail for replacement at another time.   _____

42. Juan's wrist bone is called

   A. carpus.

   B. metacarpus.

   C. digit.

   D. radius.   _____

43. Very dry cuticles may cause

   A. pterygium.

   B. onychophagy.

   C. hangnails.

   D. brittle nails.   _____

44. Darryl's hangnails are caused by

   A. a thick lunula.

   B. a thin dermis layer.

   C. an injured matrix.

   D. dry cuticles.   _____

45. The type of polish remover to use on clients who have artificial nails is

   A. acetone.

   B. nonacetone.

   C. alcohol.

   D. hydrogen peroxide.   _____

46. The radial artery supplies the

   A. thumb side of the arm.

   B. little finger side of the arm.

   C. palm of the hand.

   D. back of the hand.   _____

47. While performing a pedicure, Anita should use _____ to separate her client's toes.

    A. paper towels

    B. her fingers

    C. toe separators

    D. her orangewood stick   _____

48. When using quarternary ammonium compound, one important step is to

    A. measure it carefully.

    B. change it after each use.

    C. change it daily.

    D. dilute it to an antiseptic strength.   _____

49. The nail technician should file Tony's fingernails

    A. from center to each corner.

    B. from each corner to the center.

    C. straight across.

    D. back and forth.   _____

50. Mai uses quats to disinfect her implements. Another name for quats is

    A. sodium hypochlorite compound.

    B. formaldehyde.

    C. quaternary ammonium compound.

    D. ethyl alcohol.   _____

51. Mark is applying a form of nail art that uses very tiny rhinestones. This type of nail art is

    A. gems

    B. striping tape.

    C. foil.

    D. airbrushing.   _____

52. Tinea pedis is another name for

    A. hangnails.

    B. ingrown nails.

    C. athlete's foot.

    D. brittle nails.   _____

53. The ulnar nerve supplies the

    A. thumb side of the arm.

    B. little finger side of the arm.

    C. fingers.

    D. wrist.   _____

54. The deep fold of skin in which Mary's nail root is lodged is called the

    A. nail fold or mantle.

    B. nail groove.

    C. eponychium.

    D. lunula.   _____

55. It is important to sanitize a client's nails before applying acrylic nails because the antiseptic will

    A. adhere or attach the acrylic to the natural nail.

    B. soften the nail properly for acrylics.

    C. help retard the growth of bacteria.

    D. dry the acrylic quickly.   _____

56. Korbi is placing his manicuring implements in a disinfectant solution. The type of sanitizer he is using is a/an

    A. ultraviolet sanitizer.

    B. disinfection container.

    C. autoclave.

    D. dry sanitizer.   _____

57. The name of Tom's skin coloring pigment is

    A. lymph.

    B. keratin.

    C. sebum.

    D. melanin.   _____

58. The parts of a muscle are

    A. origin, digits, and belly.

    B. origin, insertion, and belly.

    C. digits, insertion, and phalanges.

    D. insertion, belly, and phalanges.   _____

59. Sara, a nail technician, should apply nail polish in strokes that are

    A. rough and jerky.

    B. quick and smooth.

    C. short and dry.

    D. long and excessively wet.   _____

60. Emil should store his dirty/soiled towels in _____ until he has time to launder them.

    A. a bin at the shampoo area

    B. an open container for soiled items

    C. a closed container for soiled items

    D. the manicuring drawer   _____

61. What does a disinfectant do to bacteria? It

    A. kills all bacteria.

    B. kills only pathogenic bacteria.

    C. retards bacteria growth.

    D. retards only pathogenic bacteria growth. _____

62. Ron, a nail technician, has just completed a manicure and is cleaning up his table area. Ron is to discard all of the following used items *except* the

    A. cuticle nippers.

    B. emery board.

    C. orangewood stick.

    D. cotton balls. _____

63. The nail plate is made up of a protein called

    A. collagen.

    B. melanin.

    C. keratin.

    D. sebum. _____

64. Maria's rubber implements should not be disinfected with

    A. phenolics.

    B. quaternary ammonium compound.

    C. sodium hypochlorite compound.

    D. fumigant tablets. _____

65. Nail technicians use nail forms when they apply

    A. nail tips.

    B. acrylic nails.

    C. mending tissue.

    D. acrylic over nail tips. _____

66. The nail plate, or body, extends from the nail root to the

    A. lunula.

    B. matrix.

    C. nail bed.

    D. free edge. _____

67. While nipping her client's cuticles, Lisa accidently cuts into the skin and it begins to bleed. Lisa should apply _____ to the cut.

    A. alum

    B. disinfectant

    C. 70% ethyl alcohol _____

    D. a styptic pencil

68. Lee's sudoriferous glands

    A. regulate his body temperature.

    B. are commonly known as oil glands.

    C. empty into his hair follicles.

    D. secrete sebum. _____

69. In some states, formalin

    A. cannot be used.

    B. is felt to be the safest disinfectant.

    C. is used to sanitize hands.

    D. must be FDA registered. _____

70. The nail grooves are indentations found at the _____ of the nail.

    A. base

    B. sides

    C. root

    D. free edge _____

71. The maintenance of the normal, internal stability of Ellen's body is known as

    A. homeostasis.

    B. leukonychia.

    C. carcinogenic.

    D. onychogryposis. _____

72. Carlos is putting an antiseptic on his client's nails in preparation for artificial nails.
    An antiseptic

    A. kills only pathogenic bacteria.

    B. kills only nonpathogenic bacteria.

    C. kills all bacteria.

    D. slows bacteria growth. _____

73. Sandy is preparing her client's natural nails for acrylics. Before applying the acrylic, Sandy must

    A. soften them with cream.

    B. buff them to remove the shine.

    C. soak them in hot oil.

    D. soak for 10 minutes in warm soapy water. _____

74. Sue hears, smells, tastes, touches, and sees well. Her five senses are under the control of her
    _____ nervous system.

    A. peripheral

    B. neurological

    C. central

    D. autonomic _____

75. Nails by Natalie, The Nail Clinic, and Bertha's Beauty Salon all use the same disinfection method. The most common method that salons use is _____ disinfection.

A. physical

B. steam or moist heat

C. chemical

D. autoclave

_____

SCORING

Number of Items Wrong	Score*
0	100%
1	99%
2	97%
3	96%
4	95%
5	93%
6	92%
7	91%
8	89%
9	88%
10	87%
11	85%
12	84%
13	83%
14	81%
15	80%
16	79%
17	77%
18	76%
19 or more	fail

*There are 75 items on this test. Each item is worth 1.33 points. Because of this, some percentages in the score column are missed or the score column does not list every percentage chronogically.